The Making of the Twentieth Century

This series of specially commissioned titles focuses attention on significant and often controversial events and themes of world history in the present century. The authors, many of them already outstanding in their field, have tried to close the gap between the intelligent layman, whose interest is aroused by recent history, and the specialist student at university. Each book will therefore provide sufficient narrative and explanation for the newcomer while offering the specialist student detailed source-references and bibliographies, together with interpretation and reassessment in the light of recent scholarship.

In the choice of subjects there will be a balance between breadth in some spheres and detail in others; between the essentially political and matters scientific, economic or social. The series cannot be a comprehensive account of everything that has happened in the twentieth century, but it will provide a guide to recent research and explain something of the times of extraordinary change and complexity in which we live.

The Making of the Twentieth Century

Series Editor: CHRISTOPHER THORNE

Other titles in the Series include

Already published

In preparation

Fascism in Italy: Its Development and Influence

Elizabeth Wiskemann

Macmillan

London · Melbourne · Toronto

St Martin's Press

New York

1 9 6 9

Published by
MACMILLAN AND CO LTD
Little Essex Street London w c 2
and also at Bombay Calcutta and Madras
Macmillan South Africa (Publishers) Pty Ltd Johannesburg
The Macmillan Company of Australia Pty Ltd Melbourne
The Macmillan Company of Canada Ltd Toronto
St Martin's Press Inc New York
Gill and Macmillan Ltd Dublin

Library of Congress catalog card no. 69–17733

Printed in Great Britain by
ROBERT MACLEHOSE AND CO LTD
The University Press, Glasgow

Contents

Plates and Maps

The cover picture shows Mussolini addressing workers.

PLATES
between pages 56 and 57

The author and publishers wish to thank the following for
permission to reproduce the plates: cover picture, 1*a*, 2*a*, 3*a*,
4, 5*b*, 6*a*, Radio Times Hulton Picture Library; 1*b*, 3*b*,
Associated Press; 1*c*, Arnoldo Mondadori; 2*b*, 8*a, b*, Central
Press; 5*a, c*, 6*b*, 7*b*, Mansell Collection; 7*a*, Keystone Press

MAPS

The maps are based on those in *Italy 1947* (World Today Series) by Elizabeth Wiskemann and are reproduced by courtesy of the Oxford University Press.

Author's Note. As my approach to this subject is solely European and I have no qualifications whatever to make statements about extra-European countries, the influence of Italian Fascism on, say, South America is not touched upon in this book.

Elizabeth Wiskemann

Abbreviations

E.N.I.M.S.	Ente Nazionale per l'istruzione media e superiore.
F.I.A.T.	Fabbrica Italiana Automobili Torino.
F.I.O.M.	Federazione Italiani Operai Metallurgici.
F.U.C.I.	Federazione Universitaria Cattolica Italiana.
G.I.L.	Gioventù Italiana del Littorio.
I.M.I.	Istituto Mobiliare Italiano.
I.R.I.	Istituto di Ricostruzione Industriale.
S.A.	Sturmabteilung.
S.S.	Schutzstaffel.

ITALY SINCE
NAPOLEON

Former Papal States

Former Kingdom of Naples
and Sicily, i.e. "the South"

Territory gained at the end of
the first World War

0   50   100   150   200
MILES

1 The Origins of Fascism

ITALY, united in 1870, was usually described as a liberal state. Although the constitution gave the Crown great power, the three kings, even including the first Victor Emmanuel, accepted parliamentary control in a way in which this was never accepted by the rulers in Vienna or Berlin before 1914. Italian liberalism, however, had a very narrow base. In 1882 this had been slightly broadened by increasing the electorate from 2 per cent to 7 per cent of the whole population. But Italy remained a narrow oligarchy until the circumstances of the twentieth century overtook it.

In the first fifteen years of this century, under the rule or influence of Giovanni Giolitti, who was Prime Minister for the greater part of the period, salutary changes were brought about in Italy. It was a time of economic expansion in the north, and Giolitti introduced useful social measures in conjunction with the workers' and peasants' own organizations. The devout Catholics, who had hitherto boycotted the Italian State, began to vote at elections, and in 1912 the franchise was extended so as to become almost general. 8·6 million Italians were now entitled to vote, of whom at least three million were illiterate – the illiterates had to be thirty instead of twenty-one, or else to have completed their military service. Giolitti, a Piedmontese and a liberal civil servant by training, was an excellent administrator. Without wars he might have helped to steer the liberal state through its transformation from oligarchy to democracy. Although he was sometimes high-handed and unscrupulous, in his day social progress and the co-operation of different social strata were encouraged, and there was remarkable liberty of opinion. Giolitti's mind, moreover, was sceptically open to new ideas. It is interesting that Willi Münzenberg, a young German Marxist living and working in Zürich, when he visited Italy in 1911 found young Italian officers in uniform at a Socialist meeting in Florence. As he commented, in Germany then they would not have been allowed even to read a Socialist newspaper in their barracks. This was also, however, a period of dark reactions against liberalism all over Europe, of Marxist demands for merciless revolution, of arrogant imperialistic claims, of exasperated nationalistic clashes between Germans and Slavs and Italians, even of crude racialistic ambitions here and there, particularly in Austria and Germany.

In the nineteenth century Italian nationalism had been essentially liberal, but by the twentieth it had changed. Now it remembered the Roman Empire, nurtured colonial claims upon Africa and demanded preparation for the wars these might provoke. In the writings of Enrico Corradini it found a special justification for Italian expansion by borrowing what had become a Marxist word. For Corradini claimed that Italy was a 'proletarian' nation and needed Libya in order to stop the 'haemorrhage' of emigration. Inevitably some of the entrepreneurs in Italy's new heavy industry were interested in the fabrication of weapons. Aggressive nationalism was supported, too, by the Italian Futurist movement led by Marinetti and the painter Boccioni, for they and their friends admired violence before everything, and believed war to be good social hygiene, they said. In Trent and in Trieste Italians were still ruled by Austria, and old Mazzinians envisaged war to end this.

It was particularly in the Adriatic that the atmosphere was increasingly tense in the years which led up to the First World War. The poet Gabriele d'Annunzio, born at the Adriatic town of Pescara, was the great Italian literary figure at the turn of the century and for years after that, in the van of *art nouveau*. In 1908 he published a dramatic poem called *La Nave* glorifying Venice and the Venetian Empire. This involved Italian claims, not so much to Trieste (which was Italian-speaking but post-Venetian), but rather to Istria and Dalmatia, which were also under Austrian rule. In 1907 the first Austrian elections with universal male suffrage (from the age of twenty-four) had been held, and it had become clear that, except for some of the coastal cities, Istria and Dalmatia were predominantly Slovene and Croat; only a few Italians represented them now in the Austrian Parliament. This had come as a shock to Italians in the Adriatic. They were accustomed to italianising the Slav peasantry of the Istrian hinterland. They had felt themselves to be conferring the privilege of *italianità* upon the Slovenes; indeed their attitude was rather like that of the Germans in Bohemia or the Magyars in Slovakia to the Slavs. That these Slavs should now prefer to be themselves seemed incomprehensible. At the time of the Balkan Wars Pope Pius X, who had been Patriarch of Venice, expressed much Italian feeling when he spoke of the Slavs of the Balkans as so many barbarians.

By the secret Treaty of London, signed between the Entente Powers and Italy in April 1915, the Allies promised Dalmatia as well as the Trentino, Trieste and part of Albania and Asia Minor to Italy, but not Fiume. In the early summer of 1915, when Italy came into the war on the Allies' side, Italian public opinion was sharply divided. The loudest voices came from the interventionist minority, those of d'Annunzio, the Futurists, the Syndicalists, the new Nationalist Party, but also those of the Mazzinian Republicans and other liberally-minded people. In favour of neutrality were most of the aristocracy and the Catholic hierarchy and – strange bedfellows, these – the majority of the Socialists. And Giolitti (then out of power) and his own Liberal followers were opposed to intervention, chiefly because Giolitti felt that Italy's economic advance under his recent leadership would be gravely jeopardised by war; this was only too true. After the military disaster of Caporetto in

1917, Italy triumphed in 1918 over a disintegrating Austria–Hungary.

This disintegration was partly brought about by the entry of the United States into the war in April 1917 which caused the general acceptance of the emphasis laid by Woodrow Wilson upon freedom for the hitherto foreign-ruled nationalities of Europe. Representatives of these 'oppressed nationalities', mostly the subjects of Austria or Hungary, met a congress in Rome itself in the following April. The common aims of Italians, Czechs, Slovaks, Southern Slavs, in freeing themselves from Habsburg power, were stressed.

In the autumn of 1918, when the Italians defeated the Habsburg Army at Vittorio Veneto, d'Annunzio and many of the interventionists of 1915 revived their wildest claims at the expense of the Yugoslavs in the Adriatic. Although President Wilson seemed perfectly willing that Italy should acquire the Brenner frontier, giving her over 200,000 Austrian Germans, he stood firm on the need to aim at an ethnic frontier between Italians and Yugoslavs. The Italian claim to be the heir of Venice was even historically shaky since the Venetians had not generally settled in the territories of their empire. D'Annunzio, however, raised the cry that Italy's victory was to suffer unacceptable 'mutilation', and his protests acquired fervent support among many of his compatriots.

When the Peace Conference assembled in Paris the clash between Italy's claims and the American veto intensified. During April 1919 discussion of Fiume and Dalmatia reached a climax. Moderate Italians at home thought that, in spite of the Treaty of London which Wilson would in any case not recognise, Dalmatia should be Yugoslav but Fiume Italian. Orlando, the Italian Prime Minister, inclined to this view himself although his Foreign Minister, Sonnino, strongly disagreed. However by 24 April Orlando had lost patience and the Italian delegation left Paris only to return on 5 May, weakened of course by absence. Finally, although

Dalmatia with Fiume were to go to Yugoslavia by the Treaty of Saint-Germain, Italy got Trieste with Istria as well as the Brenner frontier, a share in German reparations and a permanent seat on the Council of the League of Nations. She was thus in a strong position to carry out a successful policy of conciliating the new Slav states. In 1920, when Carlo Sforza became Foreign Minister, he aimed at this and to take Austria's place as a more benevolent patron of Yugoslavs and Czechoslovaks.

On the eve of war the Socialist peasant co-operatives in Emilia and the Po Valley had been defying the big land-owners over the supply of labour, while the poverty of southern Italy offered what seemed to be an insoluble problem. After the war the Italian Socialist Party, which always vacillates between moderation and extremism, was inspired by Russian events to make revolutionary demands both in country and town. It mocked at the intervention which had ostensibly brought so little, and thus enraged nationalistic sentiment doubly. The Nationalists gained active support from hordes of young ex-servicemen, especi-ally the black-shirted *Arditi* of the Commando units, who found it difficult to return to civilian life; they were a mixture in which former university students predominated but which included some liberated criminals.

During the war d'Annunzio had distinguished himself in the most improbable fashion. He had led air-raids on Austrian cities, upon which he dropped propaganda leaflets composed by himself; these operations had cost him an eye, but he was undaunted. In September 1919, when the Peace Settlement had awarded Dalmatia to the new Yugoslavia, d'Annunzio, marching from Ronchi with a following of a few hundred regular officers of the Sardinian Grenadiers and some *Arditi*, seized from Allied troops, and occupied, Fiume – the formerly Hungarian port which the Yugoslavs, calling it Rijeka, hoped to be about to acquire. D'Annunzio established himself there for fifteen months. He was applauded as the hero of the Adriatic, the man who did not submit to liberal governments. He was supported by the syndicalists of the seamen's union and of others. In November 1919, however, elections were held in Italy for the first time according to a system of proportional representation. From these elections, which are generally considered to have been the freest ever held in Italy until 1946, the Socialists emerged as the biggest party, and the new Catholic *Popolari*, the champions of land reform, as the second largest: there was astonishingly little support for d'Annunzio and the Nationalists. If the Socialists and *Popolari* could have co-operated, a leftist régime would have been workable: this fact was the basis of the Government of the *Centro-Sinistra* in Italy after 1963. For the intransigence of both in their determination to avoid any compromise, which they damned as worthy of the soiled hands of Giolitti, made a decisive contribution to the collapse of the liberal state. It in fact prevented the transformation of a fairly oligarchic liberalism into democracy.

A man called Benito Mussolini had been an invaluable asset to d'Annunzio and the interventionists in 1915 because he put at their disposal the daily newspaper he had recently founded, the *Popolo d'Italia*. Mussolini was a renegade Socialist, un-Marxist in temperament, although, among other things, he had read a good deal of Marx; Georges Sorel influenced him more naturally and more profoundly. His career up to this time had been restless, violent, ambitious; he was essentially subversive, it has been said. His avowed aims were obscure and variable, but he clearly thirsted for power for himself. His temperament was violent and intolerant; hence he loathed liberal doctrines. He had great journalistic facility, tinged with violence. He had grown up in the oligarchic Italy which was only superficially liberal in the 1890s – his seventeenth birthday fell in July 1900 a few days before the murder of King Umberto by an anarchist. Surprisingly this event was the prelude to the

Giolittian era of reform and economic expansion. The Giolittian era, however, brought about the triumph of the violent wing of the Italian Socialists at their congress at Reggio Emilia in June 1912. Soon after this Mussolini, prominent since Reggio Emilia, was made the editor of the Socialist newspaper *Avanti!*, sales of which went up; the invective of Mussolini was more popular than the more sober writing of his predecessors at the paper, Bissolati and Treves.

In November 1914 Mussolini was nevertheless expelled from the Socialist Party because he had declared for war. 'The Socialist Party expels you, Italy embraces you', the anti-liberal writer Prezzolini and his friends of the periodical *La Voce* in Florence telegraphed to Mussolini. Mussolini now joined with Syndicalist and Futurist groupings to form interventionist *Fasci di Azione Rivoluzionaria*.

At the end of the war he and Marinetti associated with the *Arditi* and other ex-servicemen amidst patriotic protests against the liberal state and the concessions it offered to the Slavs. His own military service gave Mussolini greater familiarity than he had had before with nationalistic slogans; *trincerismo* was one of these, meaning 'trench-mindedness'.* Then came the defeat of Caporetto for which Mussolini gladly held the parliamentary system responsible.[1] 'In the summer of 1918 he took the fateful step of accepting subsidies for his paper from big business, notably Ansaldo', the big shipbuilding firm directed by the Perrone brothers at Genoa.[2]

The Mazzinian Republicans and the moderate Socialists were rightly anxious to find a *modus vivendi* with the new Slav states, particularly with Yugoslavia; they believed that Italy should be the friend of the Slavs, indeed their leader. They thought that Fiume should be Italian but Dalmatia Yugoslav; hence the others denounced them as *Rinunciatari*, although in the case of Fiume they asked for more than the

* *Trincea* is the Italian for 'trench.'

peace settlement allowed. On 11 January 1919, when the moderate Socialist leader, Leonida Bissolati, addressed a meeting at the opera-house of La Scala in Milan in favour of conciliating Yugoslavia by accepting a Yugoslav Dalmatia, Mussolini, Marinetti and their *Arditi* followers broke up the meeting.* 'This was the first planned violence of post-war Italy.'³ Shortly afterwards, on 23 March at the Piazza San Sepolcro in Milan too, Mussolini and Marinetti founded their *Fasci Italiani di Combattimento* with a republican and syndicalist programme, a mass of contradictions, published in the following June. It contained all the revolutionary aspirations of 1919, *Diciannovismo* as they were called. The Monarchy and Senate were to be abolished. There was to be a Constituent Assembly, universal suffrage for both sexes and proportional representation. There was to be decentralisation and autonomy for the regions and communes. There were to be elected judges, as in Switzerland, and the referendum. The political police was to be abolished together with conscription. Land was demanded for the peasants, a capital levy, an eight-hour day in industry and a share in factory management for the workers, there was to be liberty of thought and the confiscation of ecclesiastical property. There was to be open diplomacy and the peoples were to be federated. This programme had been drawn up by Alceste De Ambris, one of the founders of the syndicalist *Unione Italiana del Lavoro* in 1914. Mussolini made two speeches on 23 March 1919. In the second one he claimed as his goal national syndicalism or economic democracy. 'We are strongly opposed to all forms of dictatorship'; he concluded: 'The only dictatorship we do acknowledge is that of will and intelligence.'

From now on members of the *Fasci di Combattimento* were called *Fascisti*. The word Fascio meant a 'bunch, bundle or

* Mussolini had participated in the Congress of Oppressed Nationalities in Rome in April 1918. That he now demonstrated furiously on the other side made all the more impression.

group', a *fascio di fiori*, as one can read in d'Annunzio, being the Italian for a 'bunch of flowers'. There had been vaguely socialistic *fasci* since at least 1871 when Garibaldi founded a *fascio operaio* at Bologna. Thus the word *Fascismo* in its country of origin meant very little beyond togetherness. The more classically-minded Nationalist Party liked to associate it with the severity of the symbol of the Roman lictors' *fasces* which were bundles of rods for chastisement. Quite early, although it is difficult to say exactly when, the Fascists themselves 'went Roman', using terms like 'centurion' in their formations.[4] They soon adopted the lictors' fasces too, and spoke of founding a Fascio in this sense wherever they could muster a group of supporters. But there was much variety from region to region which makes it difficult to be certain about such usages. As F. W. Deakin has said, the roots of Fascist power 'as a revolutionary movement had been in origin regional'.[5]

The Fascists' programme of 1919 praised the League of Nations, but it also glorified war and colonial expansion, and demanded the just rewards of victory. In September d'Annunzio's coup naturally aroused great enthusiasm among the Fascists, as did the claim that d'Annunzio would soon march from Fiume to purge Rome of liberalism.

In the election of November 1919 the Fascists gained no single seat and Mussolini seemed to have no future. In the next six months or so, however, his tactical hunch showed him that where d'Annunzio had in fact failed he, Mussolini, might succeed in seizing power. The condition of Fiume soon discredited the poet, but the emotions he had aroused, and the young men he had attracted, were waiting to be used. With his second wind in September 1920 d'Annunzio published his *Carta del Carnaro* (Statute of Regency) with a strongly syndicalist flavour. Indeed in Fiume he devised much of the ideology and inaugurated the whole ritual of nascent Fascism. It was he who began the orator's dialogue with the crowd, it was he who devised the plan of purging his political opponents with castor oil; the humiliation of an enemy was essential. But by the autumn of 1920 d'Annunzio had lost grip, and at the end of the year he was driven out of Fiume by the Italian government now again headed by Giolitti himself with Carlo Sforza as Foreign Minister.

Secretly Mussolini must have been glad of d'Annunzio's humiliation; he was certainly impressed by Giolitti's action.[6] During 1920 he took care to keep both the Adriatic and the syndicalist cards in his hand. In July 1920 Fascists in Trieste burnt down the Slovene headquarters there. The Fascist shock troops who did this were called *squadristi* – they had come into being in order to use violence. A month later, in reply to a lock-out in Milan, the workers of northern Italy occupied and tried to manage the most important factories, and thus the Socialists seemed on the verge of achieving their revolution, or so the young Antonio Gramsci thought.* Mussolini expressed sympathy for the workers and their syndicalist claims to a share in management. Although Giolitti's Government did not interfere for various reasons, the Socialist side wavered and then withdrew, with a promise from the employers that the workers' claims to management should be satisfied. A Socialist delegation had returned from Moscow, discouraged and discouraging, and in August the Soviet Army was beaten at Warsaw.

From this time many leading Italian Socialists abandoned their extremist position although the majority of the Socialist Party remained 'maximalist', and Gramsci's supporters at the Socialist Congress at Livorno (Leghorn) broke away to form the Italian Communist Party in the following January. Local elections held in the autumn of 1920 had shown what seemed like a political stabilisation with considerable Socialist losses. The Red danger, which had been real, ceased from now on, but the fear it had aroused could be exploited for years.

* Antonio Gramsci was an inspired young revolutionary from Sardinia educated in Turin.

In the local elections an extremist or 'maximalist' Socialist Mayor called Bucco had been elected at Bologna. When on 21 November 1920 he was to be installed at the Palazzo d'Accursio, the town hall of Bologna, the Fascists of Emilia gave notice that there would be trouble. It has never been established who fired the first shot, but a nasty clash followed with a good many casualties all round, including a lawyer called Giulio Giordani, a popular figure who had been severely wounded in the war. This affray brought into action a new category of *squadristi*, not urban but agrarian people. Two young leaders of agrarian Fascists made themselves conspicuous, Grandi of Bologna and Balbo of Ferrara. With this fresh wave of support Mussolini, hungry for power, without any principle, attracted by violence, cleverly edged round to the Right where power now accumulated. For the time being he was glad to arrange to collaborate with Giolitti in a National Bloc in the election campaign of May 1921. The National Bloc united the Liberals, Nationalists and Fascists, using the symbol of the *Fascio*, the lictors' rods; the other competitors were the Socialists, the *Popolari* and the Communists. The elections gave the Nationalists ten seats in the Chamber and the Fascists thirty-five. Here was a new instrument for Mussolini, though a less important one than *squadrismo* which was now mainly used to intimidate and destroy retreating Socialism.

To define what Fascism stood for at this juncture would be hard. It was nationalistic, it was anti-Slav, it encouraged the overflowing indignation against Socialism felt by all non-Socialists, and it supplied blackleg labour. The occupation of the factories had synchronised with agrarian strikes, particularly – as ever – in Emilia. Exasperated landowners and farmers had been delighted to use Grandi's and Balbo's *squadristi* to save the rotting harvest and to intimidate the Socialist strikers. Thus Mussolini found himself backed by the strike-breakers, both industrial and agrarian. At the end of 1920 d'Annunzio's legionaries, expelled from Fiume, had mostly joined Mussolini, who had fully exploited d'Annunzio's initiative and was to continue to do so.

At this stage, even before the election of May 1921, Mussolini, once an angry atheist, began to make conciliatory gestures towards the Catholic Church. This probably caused Marinetti to abandon his active support of Mussolini. Since 1909 Futurism had been an influential movement in Italy indeed in Europe, and Mussolini had made good use of its backing. But, apart from its praise of violence, its ideology was as unimportant to him as any other. He would certainly not give away conservative political support from Nationalists, industrialists, landowners, shopkeepers, for the sake of the Futurist intellectuals. It is to be noted that, while both d'Annunzio and Marinetti, who took their own views more seriously, were disillusioned with him, they continued to give Mussolini qualified support: it was easier to do so.

An example of Mussolini's phenomenal opportunism was provided soon after the general election of 1921 when, early in August of that year, he signed a pact of pacification with some of the labour leaders and called off the attacks of the *squadristi*; this caused friction with his rural leaders, the 'ras'* as they were called, like Grandi at Bologna or Balbo at Ferrara. By November, however, although he had said he would never agree to this, Mussolini allowed the Fascist movement to be transformed into the Fascist Party, and the *squadristi* or Action Squads began to be incorporated as the Party Militia with special uniforms, a process which was gradually completed by 1924.

To what extent was this new Fascist Party 'Fascist' in the Communist sense? To what extent was it a weapon of the new Italian large-scale capitalists used against labour, the last thing that Mussolini had originally intended it to be? If he had had any principle or prejudice it was against the capitalists, the Church and the Monarchy; all his life he abused the bourgeoisie. But it had proved irresistible to him

* This Abyssinian appellation was used with some irony.

to accept the Ansaldo money in 1918 and the applause in 1920 of indignant property-owners who feared their property was lost. Anti-Socialist outrages on the part of the *squadristi* were often encouraged by people who had much to lose, and they often subscribed to Fascist funds: they were lucky to find so brilliant an agitator with a following ready to be used. Liberals had been at least as much afraid of a Marxist revolution as they were of a Fascist seizure of power. After all Mussolini was committed to nothing and they felt that responsibility might turn him into a normal politician who would restore the reign of law; he did not seem at all averse from joining the type of coalition government habitual in Italy. After Giolitti's resignation on 27 June 1921, the Fascists saw to it that a reign of Fascist terror was kept up; it was resumed not long after the pact of pacification, in spite of it. The new Premier, Bonomi, like his successor Facta, was unable to prevent this. The chief reason was that some prefects and much of the police and Army sympathised with Fascism because it had opposed the denigration of patriotism and authority which the Socialists in their euphoric period between 1918 and 1920 had encouraged. A personal feud between the leader of the *Popolari*, Don Sturzo, and Giolitti, increased the instability of the political situation.

In the winter of 1921 to 1922 Mussolini was still an enigma which everyone could interpret as they chose. Giolitti expected to return to power, perhaps with Mussolini as a colleague. According to the Fascist programme of 1919 and later pronouncements Mussolini appeared to be hotly Republican. This created a serious difficulty for the Italian Establishment, particularly for the Armed Forces whose allegiance was directly royal. It was, indeed, not until a famous speech at Udine on 20 September 1922, the anniversary of the capture of Rome in 1870 by the King's troops, that Mussolini, even then rather grudgingly, accepted the Monarchy. Although he had been working up to this for some time the evidence suggests that he was never altogether delighted to have arrived in the position of a supporter of the Crown, but his path to power was blocked until he had. To have dropped the Republic brought him closer to the hearts of the landowners and industrialists too. Unless he had done so Victor Emmanuel could scarcely have offered him the Premiership on 28 October 1922, but as he had the Army probably desired his appointment.

Before an impressive Fascist party congress at Naples from 24 to 26 October Mussolini had planned to concentrate his Blackshirts at Perugia, immediately after the meeting at Naples, in order to bring pressure to bear upon Facta's government in Rome, but particularly upon the King. The concentration at Perugia was commanded by four Fascist leaders, ever after this known as the quadrumvirs; they were the ex-*squadrista* Italo Balbo, the ex-syndicalist Michele Bianchi and the two keen monarchists, De Vecchi and General De Bono. Meanwhile Mussolini continued to discuss all kinds of ministerial combinations. With the Fascist concentration at Perugia, the Government decided to declare a state of siege and call out the Army against the Blackshirts. However, at the very last moment on the morning of 28 October the King vetoed Facta's decision and, being informed of this, Mussolini, who had left the Naples congress early for Milan, refused to join any new government unless he presided over it. It is interesting that one branch of the Italian Freemasons (who were divided) supported Mussolini's appointment.

It is, however, misleading to suppose that Fascism, whatever it might be, had finally conquered Italy in October 1922. Mussolini was at the head of a wide coalition, which included four Liberals of different kinds and two right-wing *Popolari* as well as one Nationalist and four Fascist ministers. The anti-Fascist parties sat in the Chamber as they had been elected in May 1921. There seemed to be something of a truce, and public opinion accepted emergency measures from the new Government on the assumption that it was exerting the temporary powers of a classical dictator. The fact that Mussolini was Minister of the Interior as well as Prime Minister was in Giolitti's tradition. That he should also be Foreign Minister was a novelty but involved no obvious change before 1925. In December 1922 Mussolini appointed a new Fascist *Gran Consiglio* or Grand Council to deliberate in secret; he nominated its members and directed its work. In February 1923 he fused the Fascist Party with the Nationalists who were proving competitive, particularly in the south. In the same year Giovanni Gentile's educational reform became law; it was pleasing to the new Pope, Pius XI, because it made religious instruction compulsory in all the elementary state schools.

The obvious disadvantages of proportional representation were used to justify a new electoral law drawn up by the Fascist Minister, Acerbo. This decreed that whichever party emerged as the strongest, provided it was supported by 25 per cent of the electorate, should automatically be given two-thirds of the seats in the Chamber. The remaining third was to be distributed to the other parties in proportion to the votes. When an election was held in April 1924 the Fascist Militia thoroughly terrorised the population, nearly a third of which nevertheless voted for the anti-Fascist parties. A very determined Socialist leader called Giacomo Matteotti, a member of the moderate 'Unitary' branch of the party founded early in October 1922, had made his mark since the extremist wave of Socialism had subsided; on 30 May in the new Chamber he delivered a long speech about Fascist methods during the election campaign. He declared that the election should be invalidated. He was known to be planning a further move against the Fascists' corruption. On 10 June 1924 he was attacked by a group of ex-*squadristi*; it appears that he resisted them and was consequently murdered. One would have thought that political murders had become so common that Matteotti's death might have passed almost unnoticed except by the

Socialists. On the contrary it precipitated a crisis so acute that the King was almost obliged to dismiss Mussolini who was indirectly responsible for the murder. Not by chance has every town in Italy today its via or piazza Matteotti. His murder showed Fascism for what it was, subjection to a man who condoned the use of violence against political enemies and at the same time lied the use of violence away.

Although administrative power was in his hands Mussolini lost his confidence for months. By the end of the year he recovered it partly because of the hopeless divisions among his enemies. Most of them left the actual Chamber to form the Aventine Secession led by the radical Giovanni Amendola, but most of the Liberals disapproved of this as contrary to parliamentary principles. The King disliked the Aventine people because most of them were Republicans. The decisive voices, however, were those of the Church and of industry. The Pope expressed approval of the régime against the views of the Catholic Party, the *Popolari*, and manœuvred their leader, the priest Don Sturzo, into exile in October 1924.* After the four years of confusion at the end of the war it was not unnatural that the industrialists were opposed to another 'fresh beginning', all the more so since Mussolini had gone all out to propitiate them by reducing the State's interference in the economy brought about by Giolitti. Mussolini had been able to take this liberal action in the name of syndicalism since the syndicalists originally wished to abolish the state, administering society through the trade unions.

The resolution of the crisis was not however solely due to the mistakes and misfortunes of the anti-Fascists. When Amendola on 27 December 1924 was able to publish in his journal *Il Mondo* a statement by the Fascist Cesare Rossi, who had been involved, that Mussolini was responsible for Matteotti's murder, it is true that this seemed to come just too late. The Fascist extremists had been threatening a

* Sturzo resigned the leadership of the Party in July 1923.

'second wave' of Fascist revolution, and on 31 December, as part of their threat, thirty-three Consuls of the Fascist Militia went to Mussolini demanding all or nothing, it is said.[7] Three days later on 3 January 1925 Mussolini accordingly made his famous speech in the Chamber in which he assumed personal responsibility for all that had happened. From this time onward the other parties were suppressed, and his régime became one of permanent dictatorship or, more simply, of tyranny. The ferocious ex-railwayman from Cremona, Roberto Farinacci, succeeded Michele Bianchi as Secretary of the Fascist Party.

It was he [Farinacci] . . . who broke the original Fascist Party machine which had carried through the political revolution three years earlier. He also set the frame for the future development of the whole movement, and the effects of his draconian actions were never basically reversed. By massive purges of the membership he broke the strength of the provincial bosses and their organisations, and the political fiefs of the city states of Northern Italy, which had been the strength of the early Fascist movement, lost their independence. The elements of a centralised Party machine in Rome were now set up. It is therefore primarily due to Farinacci that the Italian Fascist Party assumed a rigid frame. His successors followed his example. The Party machine became increasingly organised on lines of military discipline, and it was the Party Secretary himself who now controlled all local appointments at all levels of the Party hierarchy, with power to dismiss any nominee. The general result of such a procedure was to replace the provincial 'tyrants' by local clans, whose existence and enjoyment of office depended on the favours of a central secretariat in Rome.'[8]

On the other hand Fascist Italy remained something of a compromise for, in spite of the Fascist programme of 1919, the Monarchy and the Senate survived. Far from the break with traditional religion which occurred in Nazi Germany, Mussolini, it has been seen, had already taken measures to conciliate the Catholic Church, and he had every intention of following up the advances made by the Italian state during the war to the Vatican in order to arrive at a settlement of the Roman Question.

The 'One-Party State' was a paradoxical novelty borrowed by Fascism from Soviet Russia. A political group, misusing the liberal conception of a free party, was able to extend its power to be equivalent to that of an absolute monarch by destroying all rivals instead of debating with them. The phraseology gave the new absolutism the appearance of popular support. By comparison with the Second Empire in France, a party myth replaced the Napoleonic one, and more attention was paid to the masses because new mass media made it possible. This and the Party Militia sharpened the shadow of Fascism, which not only penalised open disagreement in every way, but based itself upon a system of propaganda involving large-scale deception. Mussolini was aware of the similarities between Soviet Russia and Fascist Italy; indeed one feels that he was fascinated by them. The chief contrast lay in the economic absolutism of the Soviet Russian state, which had replaced the entrepreneurs and the big landowners of Russia.

[1] Cf. R. De Felice, *Mussolini il rivoluzionario* (1965).
[2] C. Seton-Watson, *Italy from Liberalism to Fascism* (1967) p. 516.
[3] Ibid., p. 518.
[4] See Italo Balbo, *Diario 1922* (1932).
[5] F. W. Deakin, *The Brutal Friendship* (1962), p. 29.
[6] R. De Felice, *Mussolini il rivoluzionano* (1965).
[7] L. Salvatorelli and G. Mira, *Storia d'Italia nel periodo fascista* (1964), p. 351, and Adrian Lyttelton in *Journal of Contemporary History*, vol. I, no. 1 (1966).
[8] F. W. Deakin, *The Brutal Friendship* (1962), p. 30.

2 The Fascist Régime: The Lateran Agreements

FROM 1925 onwards for the next three years the suppression of Italy's freely elected local bodies was carried through. Hitherto the freely elected mayors in the communes had been able to criticise the behaviour of the powerful prefects appointed by the Ministry of the Interior. Now the Ministry appointed *Podestà* to take the place of the mayors, but to say yes to the prefects, not to criticise them.

There was a curious series of curious attempts on Mussolini's life in 1926 (the first, that by Zaniboni was in fact in November 1925) culminating in that of a man with the oddly similar name of Zamboni on 31 October. These seemed to justify the 'Exceptional Decrees' of November 1926 according to which all other political parties than the Fascists were suppressed and all newspapers which did not toe the party line. The Freemasons, too, were all suppressed although one branch of them had supported Mussolini. The law was stiffened in various ways and the death penalty, which had been abolished in 1889, was reintroduced for seeking to assassinate the King or the Duce. A Special Fascist Tribunal was established, the majority of whose members must be senior officers in the Fascist Militia but need not be lawyers. Just before this, in September 1926, Arturo Bocchini was appointed Chief of the Police, and a political police force or inspectorate was developed by him which from the end of 1927 onwards was called the OVRA.* There was considerable friction between the Fascist Party

* What these letters stood for is uncertain.

and Bocchini's police. Bocchini was described by the Fascist Tamaro as 'unconvinced by Fascist notions' but certain of the necessity to protect Mussolini's life: Tamaro praised Bocchini as efficient.[1]

The Fascist system worked grimly but with judicial loopholes. Some political cases came up before the ordinary courts which were never wholly polluted by Fascism: the same could be said of the Civil Service. The Special Tribunal began to operate on 1 February 1927, but as late as September of the same year Carlo Rosselli and Ferruccio Parri, two staunch anti-Fascist Republicans, were tried by an ordinary court at Savona. They took their chance and made their trial into a magnificent indictment of Fascism. The old Socialist leader Filippo Turati, referring to the glorious 'Five Days' of Milan in 1848, called it the 'Cinque Giornate Giudiziarie'. 'Ten of these trials and the régime will be finished,' a Fascist lawyer commented, and nothing so sensational occurred again. Gramsci and batches of lesser Communists were tried by the Special Tribunal in 1927 and 1928: the Public Prosecutor demanded a twenty-year sentence for Gramsci 'to prevent this brain from functioning'. Turin had enjoyed a recent period of intellectual flowering of liberal and socialist thought. In one way or another the Fascists succeeded in destroying its two greatest political heroes, Gramsci and Gobetti. For Gramsci died in prison in 1937* and Gobetti, who was similarly frail, died from a Fascist cudgelling much earlier.†

Even the Fascist régime seldom condemned its political enemies to more than 'confino'. This involved exile to some remote island like Ustica or Lipari where conditions were wretched, but nearly everyone survived them. In Nazi Germany or Soviet Russia the chances of survival were certainly smaller. In 1943 there were far more Italian anti-

* In fact he was released three days before his death.

† Piero Gobetti died in France in 1926 at the age of 26; he had wished to be a liberal revolutionary Socialist.

Fascist leaders to take over responsibility after Fascism than there were anti-Nazi leaders in 1945 to take over in Germany after a much shorter period of Nazi rule.

Although the Italian labour movement had been strongly influenced from Germany and more often than not was dominated by the moderate reformism of the leading Milanese Socialists, it had for years contained a strong syndicalist movement derived from Georges Sorel and France. The syndicalists aimed at using a general strike, preferably violent, to destroy the state, and then to rebuild society around the trade unions (*Sindacati* in Italian). This pursuit of Guild Socialism affected the Italian Socialist movement as a whole, which, though it did not necessarily condemn the state, began to cherish the idea of self-government in industry, the workers at least to share in management. This demand had been included in the Fascist programme of 1919. The occupation of the factories in the late summer of 1920 had ended with the concession of workers' representation on the management. The workers had then withdrawn and in the confused months which followed the promises made to them were not carried out.

At the very time of the metal-workers' strike in northern Italy, that is in September 1920, d'Annunzio issued the Statute of his Regency in Fiume. The eighteenth provision of this Statute, which seems again to have been drafted by the syndicalist, Alceste De Ambris, ran as follows:

The State represents the aspiration and the effort of the people, as a community, towards material and spiritual advancement. Those only are full citizens who give their best endeavour.... Whatever be the kind of work a man does, whether of hand or brain, art or industry ... he must be a member of one of the ten corporations.

A list of these follows: industrial and agricultural labourers, technicians and managers. But 'the tenth has no special trade or register or title. It is reserved for the mysterious forces of progress and adventure.' This was, however, within three months of d'Annunzio's expulsion from Fiume where conditions had already become chaotic.

During 1921 rapturous dreams of combining the ways of medieval communes with modern syndicalism seemed to be in practical abeyance. On 21 April 1921 – this day was chosen as Rome's birthday – peasants from Lazio were conducted by Fascists to the Campidoglio and made to join in an oath promising the land to the peasants, to be their 'real, complete, definitive property'. Thus Red peasant leagues, particularly in Ferrara and Bologna, were increasingly transformed into 'Fascist Economic trade unions' (*sindacati economici fascisti*).[2] When later in 1921 the Fascist movement was transformed into the Fascist Party, the syndicalist, Michele Bianchi, was made Secretary of the Party. Shortly afterwards in January 1922 at Bologna he created the *Confederazione delle Corporazioni Sindacali* within the Party; these 'corporations' included representatives of both capital and labour. Bianchi was supported by De Ambris and Edmondo Rossoni, the leaders of the syndicalist *Unione Italiana del Lavoro* which they had founded in 1914 and resuscitated in 1918. Mussolini, whatever he might say, had been influenced by Sorel as much as by anyone, and syndicalism remained one path to power. Bianchi and Rossoni were converted by their Duce to the tenet that membership of the *Sindacati*, which were to be absorbed into the corporations, should be made compulsory by the state which would henceforth control them. In this way *Fascismo* could be made to imprison what had seemed to many its very essence, *sindacalismo*, by making it 'national'. Far from the state stepping down, as the syndicalists had planned, it took over control of all producers, though not of production.

The labour question was not seriously tackled by the Fascist Government until the beginning of 1926. In 1925 the social services of assistance for maternity and the institution of *Dopolavoro*, which provided entertainment for the workers'

leisure, were introduced. In April 1926 all strikes and lock-
outs were forbidden – the Fascist metal-workers of Brescia,
led by the future Party Secretary, Augusto Turati, had
struck for better wages early in 1925. This was an interesting
occasion because the old Socialist metal-workers' union, the
F.I.O.M., joined in and obviously still enjoyed much more
support than Augusto Turati and the Fascist strike
organizers.[3] But the prohibition of strikes was decisive in
bringing the acceptance by the employers of Fascist labour
legislation. During 1926 the Nationalist Minister of Justice,
Alfredo Rocco, together with the slightly sophisticated young
Fascist, Giuseppe Bottai, worked on the *Carta del Lavoro* or
Charter of Labour which was to create the new Fascist social
order. It was presented to the Fascist Grand Council in
January 1927 and promulgated by it on 21 April of that
year. In future the 'birthday of Rome', 21 April, took the
place of 1 May as Labour Day.

'Work in all its forms,' the *Carta del Lavoro* declared, 'is a
social duty. . . . The process of production, from the national
point of view, is a single whole; its aims are united and
identified with the well-being of the producers and the
promotion of national power.' In return for the ratification
of a number of socially accepted workers' rights, some dating
from Giolitti's day before the war, such for instance as free
Sundays, an annual paid holiday, extra pay for night work
and insurance supported by employers and employed but
only 'co-ordinated' by the state, the employers were assured
by Articles vii and ix: 'The Corporative State considers
private enterprise in the domain of production to be the
most efficient method and the most advantageous to the
interests of the nation. . . . The State intervenes in economic
production only when private enterprise fails or is insufficient
or when the political interests of the State are involved.'
There was also an ominous clause of the Charter, Article
xxiii, which laid down that employers must employ the labour allotted to them by the corporative labour exchanges and

these would always give preference to Fascists, particularly to those longest inscribed in the Party lists. A *Magistratura del Lavoro* provided a court of appeal for labour disputes.

The corporations developed very slowly. For some time there were only thirteen, but after seven years, according to a law of February 1934, twenty-two were arrived at, for the chemical trades, the clothing trades, mining and quarrying, cereals, and so on. The National Council of Corporations had been constituted in December 1929. Each corporation, in addition to representatives of employers and employed, contained three members of the Fascist Party 'to represent the public'. The General Assembly of Corporations con- sisted of about 800 members unevenly distributed among the twenty-two component bodies; they and the confederations they represented were all directly or indirectly the Duce's nominees, and the whole organisation was subject to the Minister of Corporations whose name was mostly Mussolini until 1929. From the beginning, as throughout the Fascist organism, the Fascist Party collided with the Fascist state over the corporations: Bottai, for instance, wanted the corporations to be controlled only by the state, while the Party Secretary, Augusto Turati, wished them to be based on the Party.

Mussolini, nevertheless, was tremendously proud of his corporative state. He declared that, unlike Soviet Russia which exercised only a bloody dictatorship, Fascist Italy had solved the social question of the twentieth century. Even Fascist sympathisers, Bottai in particular but also Tamaro, agree that the corporative system did not work in Italy. It added a bureaucracy of its own but it did not help produc- tion or the producers. It is true to say that on the whole the big industrialists only made gestures of submission and in fact bought their freedom from the Fascist state, which Cini called 'the last ditch of capitalism', by generous subscription to Fascist Party funds. The Great Depression did not hit Italy as severely as it hit Germany and Britain, but it hindered the corporative effort and real wages fell. It is noteworthy that when in 1930 Augusto Turati resigned from being Secretary of the Fascist Party he complained that the corporations were dominated by the employers: he also complained of corruption exactly as Matteotti might have.

From 1925 onwards Mussolini's craving for personal power became manifest; from that time onwards many Fascist sympathisers increasingly deplored the identification of the Fascist state with his person. Indeed it was a couple of years earlier that the young *squadrista* (as he had been) from Ferrara, Italo Balbo, had asked Mussolini: 'La rivoluzione è stata fatta per te solo o per tutti noi?'*4 In December 1925 ministers were made responsible to the Duce before the King, and Article 10 of the *Statuto* was abrogated so that the Chambers could no longer initiate legislation, but only the executive, in other words Mussolini, could do so.

Just as the Militia had been declared already in 1923 to be only at Mussolini's disposal, so the Grand Council became increasingly his instrument alone. Its functions were only fully defined by a law of 1928 amended in 1929. At that time it consisted of fifty-six people, but its numbers were later reduced to about thirty. It was now stated that the Chief of the Government 'calls it [the Grand Council] when he considers its meeting expedient, and he determines the agenda'. The Council, it was further stated, had to be consulted on all questions with a constitutional bearing such as 'the succession to the throne, the attributes and pre-rogatives of the crown', as well as those of the leader of the government. The King was known to feel uneasy about the undermining of his position. The one thing he fairly certainly prevented was the appearance of the fasces on the national flag after they had appeared on Italian Air Force aeroplanes.

Early in 1925, not very surprisingly, proportional repre-sentation had been abolished altogether; this was 'the burial

* Was the Revolution carried out just for you, or for all of us?

of the lie of universal suffrage'. In 1928 a new electoral law was brought forward by Mussolini according to which the corporations and certain other associations were to submit to the Fascist Grand Council 1000 names from which the Council would choose 400. This list was to be submitted to the electorate, now tailored to suit the Fascists; that is to say the vote was allowed to what were called the 'useful and active elements of the nation', men over twenty-one who paid contributions to the corporations or passed other financial tests and men between eighteen and twenty-one who were or had been married. These voters were to accept or – unthinkably – reject the list as it stood. On 16 March 1928, the Chamber accepted the new electoral law 'with perfect Fascist style' by 216 votes to 15. In the Senate Giolitti made a dignified protest, pointing out that true representation required free choice; this was excluded by the new law which thereby violated Italy's constitution according to the *Statuto*. Giolitti died a few months later – it was felt that he had vindicated himself in his old age after all. In this same year of 1928 Mussolini was at the head of seven ministries. It was time for him to tackle the Pope.

As Mussolini's power became more despotic – what he had begun to call totalitarian since June 1925 – his Party's pressure was increasingly resisted by the influence of the Vatican. Both the Fascist state and the Papacy were authoritarian but their authority clashed particularly with regard to the indoctrination of the young. When Mussolini founded the *Balilla*, the Fascist Youth Organisation, in 1926, it was bound to compete with the Catholic Scouts. The organisation of Fascist University Students competed for support with that of the Catholic Students, the *Federazione Universitaria Cattolica Italiana* or F.U.C.I. In both cases the resources of the Party, which, it has been seen, had been deliberately entangled with those of the state, were mobilised against the Catholics, and in January 1928 the Catholic Scouts were abolished.

In spite of his atheistic past it is clear that Mussolini longed to harness the Catholic Church to the Fascist state. A number of his intellectual supporters liked to trace the lineage of Fascism back to the Counter-Reformation, and notions of this kind could have their appeal to the Duce though the Council of Trent was hardly his period. He certainly looked to agreement with the Vatican to complete his ideological domination over the people of Italy and perhaps beyond the Italians. At the same time Pope Pius XI hoped that agreement would provide greater protection for the children of the Church and the enforcement of some of the Church's tenets.

At last in February 1929 the Lateran Agreements were signed. They consisted of the Treaty, or *Conciliazione*, and the Concordat. The first was a political settlement according to which a Papal State was re-established, but one of only 109 acres with St Peter's for its centre; its citizens consisted only of some hundreds of people attached to the Papal Establishment. The Treaty included a financial settlement according to which an indemnity of 1,750,000,000 lire was paid to the Pope for the various losses inflicted on him since 1870: 1,000,000,000 of this payment was made in Italian Government stock and the rest in cash.

By the Concordat Catholicism was confirmed as the religion of the state. In 1871 the Law of Guarantees had sanctioned a state veto upon the nomination of the clergy; this was revoked by the Concordat, according to which the ecclesiastical authorities only had privately to pre-notify the representatives of the state which thus retained a theoretical veto. On all marriage questions the attitude of the Church was to prevail, blocking any possibility of divorce except by ecclesiastical permission; civil marriage was no longer to be legally necessary. Religious instruction, which had been made compulsory in the elementary state schools according to Professor Gentile's reform of 1923, was now made compulsory in the secondary state schools as well, and the

Church could object to university appointments it disliked.

A very important article of the Concordat was Article 43. This declared: 'The Italian State recognizes the organizations affiliated to the *Azione Cattolica Italiana* in so far as these shall, as has been laid down by the Holy See, develop their activities outside all political parties and in immediate dependence on the hierarchy of the Church for the diffusion and realization of Catholic principles.' This statement was big with trouble for the future but scarcely affected the vital issue that Dr Binchy[5] has called the custody of the child. The rivalry between the *Balilla* and the Catholic Scouts which had occurred since the foundation of the *Balilla* had, as we have seen, caused very serious friction in the years leading up to the Concordat, and was, indeed, a weapon which each side tried to use in the preparatory negotiations. When the Pope was manœuvred into the dissolution of his scouts the *Balilla* absorbed them. It was agreed, however, that priests should be attached to the Fascist Youth Organisations which were in future to preface their activities with Catholic observances: membership of the *Balilla*, by the way, had gradually become compulsory. The Concordat was interpreted by the Catholic side as the beginning of the desecularisation, as it were, of Fascist youth. The ambiguity suited Mussolini very well: he had arranged to hold the first election on the new plebiscitary lines on 24 March 1929 in order to exploit the popular feeling of applause for the end of the *Dissidio* between Church and State which had existed since 1870. The Fascists also intended that the strongly Catholic voters should be propitiated by the, as yet, unratified Lateran Agreements.

As soon as the voting was over, and the new Chamber met, the agreements were debated in it. On 13 May 1929 Mussolini made a long and equivocal speech to the deputies which was essentially concerned to emphasise that the Fascist state was absolute and would therefore control the activities of the Church whatever was said in the Concordat.

'We have not resurrected the Temporal Power of the Pope,' he said, 'We have buried it. The régime is vigilant, nothing escapes it. . . . Let everyone remember that the Fascist régime, when it begins a war, fights it to a finish and leaves but a desert behind.' Most crucial, probably, was his claim that 'Education must belong to us: these children must, of course, be educated in our religious faith, but we need to integrate this education, we need to give to youth the sense of virility, of power, of conquest.' Fascism was determined to indoctrinate the next generation in this anti-Christian sense. If on the way it could borrow Catholic support of the anti-liberal authoritarian approach, it had every intention of doing so, stealing Catholic blessings for military exercises. The *Balilla* would see to it that even the priests of the future grew up with a sense of virility and conquest, it was hoped.

Pope Pius XI replied to this speech of Mussolini's on the following day in addressing the pupils of the Jesuit College of Mondragone. 'The state is not there in order to absorb, swallow up or annihilate the individual and the family; that would be contrary to reason and nature alike.' Mussolini replied some ten days later in a more moderate and shorter speech in the Senate, but he replied by ridiculing the family as old-fashioned and by redefining the aims of the state as 'education for war'. In spite of these polemics the Lateran Agreements were ratified in June 1929 and the bronze portals at the eastern end of the Vatican Palace were thrown open; they had been half-closed for close on sixty years.

In a sense the Lateran Accords only started a fresh conflict for they very soon disillusioned some of their keenest supporters on both sides. A crisis occurred in 1931 when in March the Fascist press began to level differing accusations of disloyalty at Catholic Action which had naturally become something of a refuge for those who found Fascism distasteful: Catholic Action did indeed appear to have become suspiciously popular. 'This was a sin against the official

unanimity on which totalitarianism bases its chief preten-
tions', Dr Binchy wrote.[6] The press offensive was followed
up by rowdy incidents, the chief sufferers being members of
the university sections of Catholic Action who were waylaid
and beaten by members of the Fascist University Youth
(*Gruppi Universitari Fascisti*) in Rome, Milan, Venice, Trieste
and elsewhere. On 29 June 1931 the Pope replied in the
Encyclical *Non abbiamo bisogno* in answer to the official
Fascist condemnation of Catholic Action issued by Mussolini
on 3 June. In the Encyclical Pius XI struck out without
reserve at the Fascist state, the attack on Catholic Action
being shown to be a move to destroy all obstacles to the
totalitarian monopoly of the souls of the young who were to
be trained in 'a pagan worship of the State'. The Pope
proceeded to condemn the oath of fidelity to the Fascist
state which Mussolini was demanding from all state officials.
Pius XI declared this oath unlawful for Catholics unless
taken with a mental reservation. 'We do not fear,' the Pope
said, 'for the fear of God casts out the fear of man.' A breach
between Duce and Pope seemed at hand.

It was of the nature of Fascism in Italy that this did not
occur. A compromise was reached early in September 1931
according to which the Catholic Youth Associations, which
had been condemned by the Government in May, were
re-allowed. But they were in future to be so decentralised
that they were bound to be far more helpless. This was a
compromise which appeared as a surrender of the Holy See
because the Italian press outside the Vatican City was
Fascist and made it seem so. Yet the very existence of
Catholic Action was a flaw in the Fascist State, and this had
been publicised in the outside world by the Encyclical
Non abbiamo bisogno. And when the Fascists said that
Catholic Action was disloyal, they were right to the extent
that some real opposition to Fascism in Italy grew out of it
with time.

What other cares had Mussolini in this period? In 1927

he had fixed the lira at ninety to the pound sterling (*quota novanta*) which was criticised as too low. In 1929, when the banks ran into difficulties after Black Friday on Wall Street, the Fascist state took them over. Late in 1931 it set up the *Istituto Mobiliare Italiano* (I.M.I.) to subsidise banks in giving credit. It also acquired considerable control over industry through the founding in January 1933 of the state-holding company, the *Istituto di Ricostruzione Industriale* or I.R.I. The slump was met, as elsewhere, by lowering salaries and wages. By and large, with the years, and partly on account of the régime's interest in armaments, the big firms grew into monopolies which dominated the corporations thus stunted in their growth: Montecatini, the great chemical firm, was an instance of an enterprise that was able to buy up all its competitors. Fascism, which had talked so much of the state not interfering as it had in Giolitti's days, now interfered overwhelmingly. And Fascism, which had talked so much of social justice, increased indirect taxation. At first the workmen, according to their Socialist traditions, found ways of protesting, but as time went on and Bocchini perfected his police machine (this was one of the things which did work well in Fascist Italy) all protests were stifled.

On the other hand it is interesting that when Augusto Turati had resigned as Secretary of the Party in 1930 he complained, among other things, that not enough was being spent on armaments and too much on public works. Here clearly there was a difficult clash within Fascism. But the improvement of certain regions of Italy was one of Fascist Italy's few undisputed successes, perhaps the only one. From 1929 to 1935 it was in the charge of an able specialist called Arrigo Serpieri, and it is recorded that up to 1933 5,270,000,000 lire had been spent on this. The draining of the Pontine marshes was entrusted to the Veterans' Association, the *Opera nazionale combattenti*, whose members were to acquire farming plots on the land reclaimed. Between November 1931 and the end of the operation, about 3000 farms were established in this formerly malarial district between Rome and Terracina. The town of Littoria (celebrating the lictors) was founded in 1932 and others followed: the province of Littoria – now Latina – was founded in September 1934. The first new settlers here came from Emilia and Venetia. Fanfares of propaganda accompanied Mussolini's public works and he took care to be photographed participating in them. Whether in relation to the period in which he lived Mussolini achieved more than Giolitti, under whose rule the trains had just as often run on time, it is hard to say. The techniques of Fascist publicity were perhaps well suited to push something like the draining of the Pontine marshes, and their proximity to Rome made them a splendid because conspicuous advertisement. The new settlements here were the nearest thing Fascism ever achieved to the oath of Rome's birthday in 1921 that the land should be given to the people.

As for Fascist insistence upon autarchy, this was part of the preparation for war. The 'battle of the grain', which Mussolini declared was to liberate Italy from 'slavery to foreign bread', was begun in 1925 and was carried on for the following seven or eight years. The effort made was to increase productivity, especially in wheat, rather than to extend the area growing it. Some success was achieved, though naturally some follies were perpetrated. However, with a growing population Italy was obliged to continue to import wheat or give up eating bread and spaghetti – not even Mussolini dared to ban spaghetti.

His attempt to increase the birth rate was unsuccessful, that is to say births increased but at a lower rate than before. Here his failure was merciful, since success could only have further reduced the standard of living and have increased the underemployment on the land, unless it had been accompanied by large-scale industrialisation which would have made nonsense of Fascist condemnation of urban life. To the solution of the chronic problem of the *Mezzogiorno*, its poverty and illiteracy, the Fascists contributed nothing but to chase the Mafia to the United States, an achievement not to be entirely despised.

[1] A. Tamaro, *Vent'anni di Storia, 1922–43* (1953).
[2] L. Salvatorelli and G. Mira, *Storia d'Italia*, p. 215.
[3] Ibid., pp. 370–1.
[4] Quoted by Tamaro, op. cit.
[5] D. A. Binchy, *Church and State in Fascist Italy* (1941), ch. xv.
[6] Ibid., p. 510.

3 Doctrine and Education

It had been asked again and again what Mussolini's doctrine really was, and the quarrel with Catholic Action in 1931 made some answer almost imperative. The opportunist Mussolini, who had changed his views so often, naturally postponed any definition as long as he could. At last in vol. xiv of the *Enciclopedia Italiana*, published in June 1932, there appeared at the beginning of the long piece on *Fascismo* the heading 'Doctrine' divided into (1) Fundamental Ideas and (2) Political and Social Doctrine.

The Fundamental Ideas are generally attributed to the philosopher, Giovanni Gentile, who had been Mussolini's first Minister of Education; the essay was very Hegelian.

The man of Fascism [it was stated] is the individual who is nation and fatherland, which is a moral law, binding together individuals and the generations into a tradition and mission, suppressing the instinct for a life enclosed within the brief round of pleasure in order to restore within duty a higher life free from the limits of time and space; a life in which the individual, through the denial of himself, through the sacrifice of his own private interests, through death itself, realizes that completely spiritual existence in which his value as a man lies. . . . Fascism is opposed to Democracy, which equates the nation to the majority; nevertheless it is the purest form of democracy if the nation is conceived, as it should be, qualitatively and not quantitatively, as the most powerful idea (most powerful because most moral, most coherent, most true) which acts within the nation as the conscience and the will of a few, even of one, which ideal tends to become active within the conscience and the will of all – that is to say of all those who rightly constitute a nation by reason of nature, history or race. . . . Not a race, nor a geographically determined region, but as a community historically perpetuating itself, a multitude unified by a single idea which is the will to existence and to power: consciousness of itself, personality. . . .

Fascism indeed is not only a law-giver and founder of institutions, but something that educates and promotes spiritual life.

The second part, 'Political and Social Doctrine' was more chaotically Mussolinian, giving his own account of the development of Fascism which was traced back to Sorel, Péguy, Lagardelle, Olivetti, Orano and Enrico Leone – at this stage there was no thought of the Counter-Reformation. With pride Mussolini then quoted from one of his speeches at the San Sepolcro meeting of March 1919 appealing to the meeting to accept 'the claims of national syndicalism from the economic point of view'. Here his article breaks off to comment on the constant occurrence of the word 'corporation' which 'in the course of the Revolution was to signify one of the legislative and social creations at the basis of the régime'.

He proceeded to boast that Fascism in its early days had had not a doctrine but faith, and that its doctrine had then followed spontaneously, self-creative, in the laws of 1926, 1927 and 1928. 'Before everything', Mussolini said, 'Fascism believes neither in the possibility nor in the utility of perpetual peace. . . . Only war brings all human energies to a maximum tension and imprints a mark of nobility upon the peoples who have the virtue to face it.'

Fascism, Mussolini rather ominously stated, was opposed to internationalistic constructions, adding a word which points this sentence in hostility at the League of Nations. He praised the proud motto of *Me ne frego** as a call to combat and stated that society required severity, distinctions and differentiations. Fascism was the negation of materialistic socialism because it believed in saintliness and heroism, that is in action into which economic motives do not enter. Nor did Fascism accept the idea of the class war and the goal of human happiness as preached in the eighteenth century. A

* 'I don't care a damn', but it is really stronger.

quotation from Renan emphasised the importance of an élite.

'The Fascist state', said Mussolini, 'organizes the nation, leaving adequate margins for the individuals; it has limited useless or harmful liberties, preserving essential ones. The judge in these matters cannot be the individual but only the state.'

At this point Mussolini directly tackled the relationship of Fascism to religion. Fascism, he said, does not create its own deity like Robespierre, nor does it, like the Bolsheviks, vainly attempt to abolish the idea: Fascism respects the God of the ascetics, the saints, the heroes and also the God to whom the simple people offer their prayers.

Finally Mussolini defined the Fascist state as a will to power and empire involving effort and sacrifice though perhaps no territorial gain. Fascism, Mussolini was convinced, was the doctrine *par excellence* of the twentieth century, when the peoples thirst for authority and order.

Some of this was a curious and not very welcome reply to the Pope. It contained also a hasty, rather embarrassed justification of the Fascist change from republicanism in 1922, a justification that did little to flatter the Monarchy, forms of government being shown to be unimportant in the long run.

So this was Fascism by 1932. The syndicalist message now seemed underplayed. Mussolini may have considered that enough had been said five years earlier in the *Carta del Lavoro*. Yet if his corporate state was the practical solution of the modern social question, the reply to Moscow, it seems strange that so much emphasis should now be laid on the spiritual character of the Fascist state – this was in fact the reply to Catholic Action.

The other extraordinary omission from 'Doctrine' in 1932 was any reference to the Fascist Party. Increasingly Mussolini played up the state which was Fascism, and vice versa Fascism was the state that squeezed the Party out. Actually a late Statute of the Fascist Party was published on 12 November 1932. It proclaimed in its first article: 'The

National Fascist Party is a civilian militia in the service of the Fascist state.' And in its twentieth: 'The Fascist who is expelled from the Party must be expelled from public life.' The new statute placed enormous responsibility upon the Secretary of the Party, who was in fact the Duce's deputy in handling the Grand Council and the other administrative Councils (including that of the corporations); similarly he was Mussolini's deputy in dealing with the Federal Secretaries of the Party below him. It would have appeared that, as the power of the Duce swelled to semi-divine proportions, that of the Secretary of the Party would do the same. This, however, was not the case. The opposite was true. Increasingly Mussolini showed a preference for weak subordinates who would not criticise. An arch-example was Achille Starace, who was made Party Secretary in 1931 in succession to Giovanni Giuriati, and who lasted until 1939. Tamaro's far from hostile attitude towards Mussolini allowed him to condemn the appointment of Starace.

In 1932 ten years of the Fascist régime was duly celebrated in the so-called *Decennale*. Mussolini made speeches all over the country foreseeing the triumph of Fascism throughout Europe. He achieved a rather childish act of defiance of the Vatican by having a statue of Anita Garibaldi set up on the Janiculum on 4 June 1932 in the presence of the King. On this occasion he declared that his Blackshirts followed the same line as Garibaldi and his Redshirts. Typical of this same period is the salutation to Augusto Turati who had joined the staff of the *Stampa* but left it in August 1932. 'We salute Augusto Turati in virile fashion, turning our thought towards Him who knows and sees everything, to Him who reads with a clear eye in the hearts of men.' As Salvatorelli adds, the paper was referring not to God but to Benito Mussolini.[1]

It is evident that education is fundamental to the totalitarian conception, for the indoctrination of the young is essential long-term investment. In Mussolini's first coalition government the most interesting figure was the formerly

Liberal philosopher, Giovanni Gentile, the 'Actual Idealist' who later formulated the first part of Mussolini's Fascist doctrine. In 1923 Gentile put through a series of laws on education that were named after him. Briefly the Gentile reform increased state control of the schools (partially centralised in 1911) but introduced greater choice of subject. By 1924 Gentile was out of office and within two more years the creation of the *Balilla* organisation for the indoctrination of the young had been worked out. It became compulsory for young Italians between the ages of four and eighteen to pass through three stages of Fascist indoctrination (as *Figli della lupa* from four to eight, in the *Balilla* from eight to fourteen, and as *Avanguardisti* from fourteen to eighteen), not at school but in their supposedly free time. They were subjected to powerful injections of patriotic exaltation all associated with the apotheosis of the Duce and the glorification of war. Girls were enrolled as well as boys, though on a smaller scale. Gentile had enforced religious instruction in the elementary schools in 1923, and in 1929 the Concordat imposed the same obligation on the secondary schools. This Catholic teaching must often have been flatly contradicted by what was taught, probably with more verve, in the *Balilla* organisations in the later part of the same day. There was certainly confusion and sometimes friction, but there was no further definition until 1939.

Meanwhile the most ingenious school textbooks were contrived under the aegis of the Fascist authorities. In the elementary schools each class had one general textbook, the *libro unico*, which was a reading-book to cover all subjects and even include religious instruction. The *libro unico* published in 1932, the year of Mussolini's definition of *Fascismo* in the Enciclopedia, for the fourth elementary class, that is for children of about ten years old, contained among other things, but as if by chance, a short life of Benito Mussolini up to his appointment by the King in October 1922. There was a glowing account of his mother, both pious and intelligent, and of the sympathy between her and Benito. Later he had gone to Switzerland to enrich his experience and pursue his studies. Later still at Trent, together with Cesare Battisti he had 'defended the *italianità* of the Trentino'. He alone had led Italy into the war. Then he was promoted corporal because 'Benito Mussolini was always the first in undertakings of courage and audacity'. After the joys of victory Italy was denied even what had been promised to her. But Mussolini of course did not despair, although he was alone but for a handful of *Arditi*. At last, after three long years of suffering, the army of the Black Shirts moved on 28 October 1922 and the King 'invited the Duce to assume the government'. The Duce then said to the King that he brought him the Italy of Vittorio Veneto which meant 'the holy young who have died for Italy and who are ready to die for her'.

Before this there were accounts of Fascist martyrs provided in the narrative of a character called Signor Lucio who also praised the King. Here was included a seductive paragraph headed *Libro e Moschetto* with an eloquent illustration of a gun laid across a book and with rather an air of *art nouveau* even so late. At the end of a paragraph about the blindness and poverty of ignorance the Duce's doggerel 'Libro e moschetto, fascista perfetto'* was quoted. This book seemed obsessed, too, with sailors and the sea, the Roman Mediterranean and so on; a bit surprisingly Emerson was quoted as saying that the most advanced nations are those that go most to sea.

Almost more creative of atmosphere was the *libro unico* published in 1932 for the fifth class of the elementary schools. It was called *Il Balilla Vittorio* and was by a former Nationalist, now of some eminence in the Fascist Party, called Roberto Forges-Davanzati. It wove patriotism, Catholicism and Fascism into a mystical whole. Vittorio is taken to Assisi by his uncle in a family party. There they meet a Franciscan monk who tells them that the convent was

* A book and a gun make a perfect Fascist.

restored to his order by Mussolini. This was all part of the Duce's preparation already in 1926 for the *Conciliazione*. 'We Franciscans', he says, 'pray every day for the Duce's well-being which is the well-being of Italy', and they feel that St Francis inspired Mussolini in his gestures to the Church. As the visitors gaze across at Perugia the monk equates the words of the Duce with the voice of God. The narrator goes on to point out that Italians are feeling a new communion 'in the immortal words of the wholly Italian saint (Francis), in the work of the Duce always present to good men. They are the Italians of this new order which is *Fascismo*, of this new Italy which after centuries of slavery ... is today the Italy of the Italians.' A little later Mussolini is described distributing parcels to children in the poor quarters of Rome: 'And the Duce smiled all the time at the children whom he loves above all, because with these children, consoled, aided, educated by Fascism, he feels sure of Italy's future.' There are longer passages, too, all describing Mussolini as something between Jesus Christ and Julius Caesar.

Land reclamation was in full swing at the time of the writing of this text book, and a chapter is devoted to it. 'Fascist land reclamation,' an engineer says to Vittorio and his brother Venanzio, 'is not only defence against malaria which has depopulated our country ... and poisoned the race. It is also the new duty of the State ... Fascist land reclamation is one of our major tasks, perhaps the most important part of that mobilisation in peace which Mussolini has known how to demand of all the Italians in the same spirit of the intervention in the war, in the spirit of the trenches and in that of victory.' An important part of Fascist – as of Communist – technique was to confuse military conceptions with peaceful ones. The remarkable prominence of the royal family in these textbooks and similar publications was a boost for the Army, perhaps, though the Queen and the Princesses were nearly as prominent as the uniformed King and Prince and their cousins.

In 1936 Giuseppe Bottai was made Minister of Education. He was one of the more interesting Fascist figures, originally a futurist and thus something of an intellectual contrasting sharply with the crude ferocity of a Farinacci. He had fought in the war, then become a *squadrista* who helped to found the Rome Fascio in 1919. It has been seen that he contributed to the construction of the corporate state, into which at one point he tried unsuccessfully to introduce appointments by free election, and to the formulation of the *Carta del Lavoro*. All along, in addition, he edited a review in Rome with, in Farinacci's view, the paradoxical title of *Critica Fascista*. In it he made 'obstinate and not entirely forlorn attempts to enunciate a "moderate" programme for a triumphant Fascism, of fundamental reform by legal revolution, achieved and modified by constant self-criticism and revision within the élite of the Party.'[2] 'I pleaded for an opposition on interior lines', he was later to write.[3] The

weakness of his case was that the essential problem created by the occupation of the state machine by Fascism – namely the demarcation of the frontiers between illegality and legitimacy in the exercise of power – could never be faced owing to the limits, both in terms of brute strength and moral ascendancy ... of the very Fascist movement itself. Between the ultra-revolutionary conception of Farinacci and the 'slow but sure revolution' by legal means of Bottai, developed the personal dictatorship of Mussolini.[4]

It must be recorded in Mussolini's favour that he made Bottai Governor of Rome in 1935, a position to which an imperial prestige, as it were, was attached. On the other hand it must be noted that a week or so before this appointment Farinacci had again been named a member of the Grand Council.

When in the following year Bottai went to the head of the Ministry of National Education he may have felt that he had more to contribute to the Fascism of the next generation than to that of his own. By February 1939 he had worked out another Charter germane to the Fascism of the future, the *Carta della Scuola*. By 1937 all the Fascist youth organisations to which one belonged up to the age of eighteen, hitherto collectively called the *Opera Nazionale Balilla*, had received the new and impressive name of *Gioventù Italiana del Littorio* or G.I.L. This was now to include the eighteen- to twenty-one-year-olds who were called *Giovani Fascisti* unless they went to a university in which case they were equally compelled to join the *Gruppi Universitari Fascisti* or G.U.F. The *Carta della Scuola* now drew the logical conclusion and fused education in school with that provided outside school by the Party. It declared:

In the Fascist order, the scholastic and political age coincide. School, G.I.L. and G.U.F. together form one instrument of Fascist education. The obligation to frequent them constitutes the scholastic service which is undertaken by the citizen from his earliest age up to twenty-one years. (Declaration ii)

Access to studies and the further pursuit of them are regulated solely according to the capacity and attitude demonstrated. . . . The State colleges guarantee the continuation of the studies of capable, not of well-to-do, young people. (Declaration iii)

From the elementary school upwards, practical work is to have its part in every curriculum. Special shifts of work, regulated and directed by the scholastic authority, in workshops and in laboratories, in the fields, on the sea, are conducive to a social and productive consciousness fitting to the corporative order. (Declaration v)

Neither the availability of continued studies regardless of means nor the practical work in the schools materialized in the short time left to the régime. Indeed only Declaration xxvi, which had been anticipated in a decree issued eight months earlier, was carried out. This established the *Ente Nazionale per l'istruzione media e superiore* (E.N.I.M.S.) as 'the organ of propulsion, co-ordination and control of all non-Royal (i.e. non-state) schools'. The E.N.I.M.S. in fact took control over the last private schools, mostly convents, whose independence had been cherished by the Catholic Church.

Since the days of the *Arditi* and d'Annunzio youth had been glorified in the potentially Fascist world, and the hymn of the movement inherited from the *Arditi* was *Giovinezza* which spoke of youth as the spring-time of beauty. For many years school children, but perhaps most of all university students, were ardent enthusiasts for the Fascist régime. The culmination of the training of the young was, in theory at least, reached at the age of twenty-one, when they completed their para-military training. Each spring there occurred the *Leva Fascista* at which ceremony the twenty-one-year-olds were received into the Party with suitable Fascist rites.

Part of the fun of being a young Fascist was that the Fascist authorities egged one on to criticise one's schoolmasters or university professors if they lacked enthusiasm for the Party. The student journal called, thanks to Mussolini's doggerel, *Libro e moschetto : Fascista perfetto*, furiously criticised the surviving liberalism of some professors. There was, indeed, a noticeable residue of liberal attitudes among the senior members of the universities. Already in 1931 the régime attacked this by imposing an oath upon every professor in the state universities as a civil servant – according to the Gentile reform the few others, the 'free' universities, such as the Catholic University of Milan, had been subjected to state control. It is interesting that Gentile himself was eager for this oath to be imposed. The professors were required to swear fealty to 'the King, his successors and the Fascist régime'. There were some men of great distinction, Lionello Venturi, Gaetano De Sanctis, Francesco Ruffini and his son, who refused the oath, and left their jobs; members of the G.U.F. demonstrated noisily against Professor Ruffini senior in Turin, but there were other students who made clear their loyalty to him. The big majority of university teachers was not, however, in a position to resign. This meant that those who should have been the intellectual leaders of society were fairly effectively shackled by the Fascists, with the exception of Benedetto Croce and a few people more or less associated with him.

In his reply to Gentile's verbose and mystical Manifesto of the Fascist Intellectuals in spring 1925 Croce described Fascism as 'an incoherent and bizarre mixture of appeals to authority and demagogy, ... unbelief and toadying to the Catholic Church, flight from culture and sterile reachings towards a culture without a basis, mystical languours and cynicism'. In 1929 Croce was the only Senator who spoke against the Lateran Agreements. He was an uncompromising anti-Fascist. And yet throughout the Fascist period he was able to publish liberal history books and his occasional literary review, *La Critica*, while his publisher, Laterza of Bari, was not afraid to do his part. It is not clear whether Mussolini countenanced this because he despised a professional philosopher and his disciples, or whether he attached propagandistic value to preserving the freedom of a man of so great an international reputation. Probably both motives operated. This was possibly the biggest gap in Fascist totalitarianism. For Croce's influence was far from negligible. In October 1929 Mussolini had set up his own Academy at the beautiful palace of the Farnesina in Rome (now the Foreign Office). Marinetti belonged and Pirandello, but little was achieved in the long run, whereas around Croce in Naples the liberal spirit survived and encouraged younger men to think further than Croce's desire to revive the past. It is difficult to guess what either Stalin or Hitler would have done with a Croce.

It may be considered that Mussolini, whose forty-ninth birthday fell just after the publication of his article in the *Enciclopedia Italiana*, was then at the height of his power and popularity. But even then it was felt by many of his official supporters that he was undertaking far too much, and enjoying too much public adulation. In September 1929 he had handed over six ministries to their under-secretaries, retaining only the Ministry of the Interior. But, like all such changes, he regarded this only as a 'changing of the guard' and soon overcharged himself again. Part of the Dictator's weakness was that he remained first and foremost a journalist, which did not make for efficient government. Temperamentally Mussolini was unable to delegate, and pro-Fascist critics like Tamaro and Bottai agree that in his twenty-one years – or rather eighteen and a half – of absolute power he failed to train any deputy leaders, still less to found an able Fascist hierarchy.

On 25 March 1934 a second plebiscitary vote for a new Chamber took place. In 1929 there had been a 'No' vote of 1·57 per cent; now this was reduced to 0·15 per cent partly perhaps because the voting-papers destroyed any secrecy of voting that had remained. The Chamber in any case had lost any meaning since Mussolini had announced that it would be replaced by the Assembly of the Corporations. Just before the so-called election on 19 March the Duce made a speech in which he declared that anti-fascism was finished but that the great danger to Italy was the 'spirito borghese', the 'bourgeois' spirit, which made for comfort and compromise. From now on this assumption of his, which was not at all new, became something of an obsession.

Two further characteristics of Fascist Italy require to be mentioned. In addition to the increase of Party oratory from Mussolini and the Party *gerarchi* (hierarchs), the practice of demonstrations by uniformed groupings in large masses grew: the black uniforms were more and more in evidence.

In 1926 a Fascist calendar had been adopted. This became obligatory in the following year. Then on 29 October 1933 Starace proclaimed the opening of the year XII of the E.F. or *Era Fascista*. The months were not interfered with.

Other changes at about the time of the *Decennale*, or soon after it, need to be recorded here. Already in July 1932 Mussolini resumed direct control of the Italian Foreign Office with Suvich as his Under-Secretary. This meant the eviction of his old collaborator, the former 'Ras' of Bologna, Grandi, who was sent to be Ambassador in London. In November 1933 much the same happened to Balbo: Mussolini himself replaced him as head of the Italian Air Ministry and Balbo was sent to succeed Badoglio as Governor of Libya. Grandi and Balbo were, by early Fascist measure, two of the ablest 'ras' there had been, and when their local power was crushed by Farinacci, Mussolini had rewarded them with high office. But both of them, though true to his cause certainly for years to come, were people who occasionally criticised and were not blindly obedient to the Duce. By now he was unwilling to hear any criticism even from his early supporters. The syndicalist quadrumvir, Michele Bianchi, had died in office at the Ministry of Public Works in 1931.

Instead of Grandi and Balbo, the young Galeazzo Ciano, son of another leading Fascist, the Duce's prospective heir, Costanzo Ciano, became increasingly prominent. After being Italian Consul in China, in 1933 Galeazzo Ciano was put in charge of the Duce's Press Office. Soon after the election of 1934 he was nominated Under-Secretary at the Press and Propaganda Office directly under Mussolini. Galeazzo Ciano was in 1934 only thirty-one: in 1930 he had married the Duce's eldest and favourite child, Edda. Thus, as Salvatorelli and Mira say, a dynastic air began to pervade the Palazzo Venezia where Mussolini worked.

To what extent had Mussolini established totalitarian rule? It has been pointed out often enough that the survival of the Monarchy and a Senate, although more than half filled with Fascist nominees, provided a brake. So did Pope Pius XI in the thirties – having decisively helped Mussolini to become Italian dictator in the previous decade. Some of the university professors who refused to take the oath of loyalty in 1931 were able to survive in Italy, in addition to the privileged Croce. Parri and his friends, Ernesto Rossi and Riccardo Bauer, were, it is true, in and out of *confino* or prison. But Luigi Einaudi, a professor in Turin and a Senator, made little secret of his liberal sympathies for which he was never penalized. He acted throughout the Fascist period as correspondent of the liberal *Economist* in London. He also edited a review in Turin called *Riforma Sociale*, which was suppressed in 1935 but restarted rather more cautiously the next year as the *Rivista di Storia Economica*.

It has been said that Einaudi's chief anxiety was for his son Giulio, now the head of the famous publishing house which he had already founded. Giulio Einaudi was the moving spirit of a leftist literary review called *La Cultura* which he brought out in Turin, and with which several eminent anti-Fascists, Salvatorelli himself and the writer Cesare Pavese were associated. *La Cultura* was suppressed in 1935, but the Einaudi publishing firm continued. Writers as different as Montale and Moravia survived the Fascist period without penalty, although Moravia's novel *Gl'Indifferenti* of 1929 was anything but Fascist in character. In fact, although Fascist pressure seemed to be constantly intensified, forces adverse to the Fascist state counteracted it in slight but real measure. Young men, who had been enthusiasts for what they had regarded as the revolutionary programme of Mussolini earlier, now formed groups to work against Fascism from within – Ruggero Zangrandi[5] has described such activities. It was only in 1939 that the apparatus of Mussolini's corporate state was completed with the *Carta della Scuola*, and with the Assembly of Corporations more or less replacing the Chamber of Deputies. The Axis alliance was discrediting Mussolini by this time, and the Second World War was looming on the horizon.

[1] Salvatorelli and Mira, *Storia d'Italia*, p. 535.
[2] F. W. Deakin, *The Brutal Friendship*, p. 48.
[3] G. Bottai, *Vent'anni e un Giorno*.
[4] F. W. Deakin, op. cit., p. 49.
[5] R. Zangrandi, *Il lungo viaggio attraverso il fascismo* (1962).

ITALY

ALBANIA

SARDINIA

MEDITERRANEAN SEA

SICILY
Malta
Pantelleria

Dodecanese & Rhodes

CRETE

TUNISIA (FRENCH)

Tripoli

TRIPOLITANIA

CYRENAICA

LIBYA

EGYPT

Suez

RED SEA

SUDAN

pre-Fascist Colonies

Fascist acquisitions

ERITREA

Massawa

Adua

Assab

FRENCH SOMALILAND

Jibuti

Gulf of Aden

BRITISH SOMALILAND

ABYSSINIA

ITALIAN SOMALILAND

Mogadishu

INDIAN OCEAN

ITALIAN
EMPIRE
UNDER MUSSOLINI

0   500   1000

MILES

4 Foreign Policy up to the Spanish Civil War

FOREIGN policy comprised a singularly important part of Fascism, which deplored peace for any length of time and praised imperial expansion. Although about half a million Slovenes and Croats in Istria had fallen to Italy in 1919 Mussolini would scarcely forget the Italian claim to Dalmatia. Nor was East Africa forgotten. In his first speech in the Chamber of Deputies after he had been appointed Premier and Foreign Minister, that is on 16 November 1922, he chose to say:

Foreign policy is the area which especially preoccupies us. . . . The fundamental guiding-lines of our foreign policy are the following: – treaties of peace, whether good or bad, must be carried out once they have been signed and ratified. A self-respecting state can have no other doctrine. Treaties are not eternal; they are not irreparable. They are chapters of history, not its epilogue. To carry them out means to test them. If, in the course of their application, their absurdity becomes evident, this will constitute the new fact that should lead to a further examination of the [signatories'] respective positions. . . .
    Just as Fascist Italy has no intention of tearing up the peace treaties, so for political, economic and moral reasons, she has no intention of abandoning her war-time allies. Rome is on the side of Paris and London.

This was late in the year of the Conference of Genoa and the Russo-German Treaty of Rapallo*: it was the year of the murder of Rathenau and the collapse of Germany's currency.

* To be distinguished from the Italo-Yugoslav treaty signed at the same place in 1920 and ratified early in 1921; see below, p. 50.

And for the time being these remarks of Mussolini's were not misleading. In the transitional period of European history which stretched to the Locarno Agreements, Mussolini did not appear to stray far from the path of Sforza.

On 27 August 1923, however, when the representatives of the Conference of Ambassadors were delimiting the Greco-Albanian frontier, the Italian representative, General Tellini, and his colleagues were assassinated; it has never been established exactly by whom. This gave Mussolini, who, it has been seen, was his own Foreign Minister, a marvellous opportunity to display the Fascist spirit. An ultimatum was despatched to Greece rather in the tone of the Austrian ultimatum to Serbia in 1914. Although the Greek reply was conciliatory, the Italian fleet, already concentrated at Taranto for possible anti-Greek action – there had been anti-Italian incidents in Greece – attacked and occupied Corfu on 31 August. Greece appealed to the League of Nations which condemned Italian aggression. The crisis was a sensational one. In the end Greece paid the compensation Mussolini had demanded to the Conference of Ambassadors, and the Italians evacuated Corfu on 27 September. For the next two years Mussolini's foreign policy was again prudent, seeming to defer to Contarini, the administrative head of the Italian Foreign Office, and to Contarini's staff.

Under cover, as it were, of the Corfu crisis Mussolini sent an Italian general to Fiume on 17 September – negotiations with the Yugoslavs over the frontiers of the Free State of Fiume, arranged for at Rapallo after d'Annunzio was expelled, had broken down. The Yugoslav was kept separate from the Greek affair and Mussolini finally came to terms with Belgrade in January 1924 by a treaty signed in Rome. The city of Fiume became Italian while the rest of the territory of the Free State went to the Yugoslavs. This was an easy success because Yugoslavia was unable to offer much resistance, and because the Serbs – including King

Alexander, who dominated policy – did not care very much about Fiume. Thus Mussolini had a striking success in foreign policy before he had been in office a year and King Victor Emmanuel obligingly gave him the Order of the Annunziata. At that time it did not suit Mussolini to intrigue with the Croats, who were sensitive about Fiume because they regarded it as theirs.

It was only after the Locarno Treaties in 1925 failed to guarantee the Brenner frontier that Mussolini became more restless. Until then the Italian Foreign Office under Contarini as Secretary-General had found him an apparently docile pupil. Its members did not know that he quickly introduced secret agents of his own to cross their plans. Always the irregular, the arbitrary, the personal, appealed to him, his own indiscipline. By this time the basis of his power at home had changed, for it was the Fascist Party and no other, strengthened by the Militia and Bocchini's police and the Special Tribunal. Until 1925 Mussolini remained on reasonably good terms with France and Britain, joined them in coming to Austria's financial rescue and seemed friendly with both Yugoslavs and Czechs.

It was in 1925, however, that Mussolini became the possessive patron of Albania. By July 1926 he was able to tell Victor Emmanuel that the Albanian chief, Zogu, was 'acquired for Italy', and an Italo-Albanian pact of friendship and security was signed at Tirana on 27 November 1926. Albania was made into an economic dependency of Italy. Inevitably relations between Italy and Yugoslavia deteriorated in consequence. Deliberately Mussolini now developed a policy in direct contradiction to that of Sforza. For he quarrelled with the Slav states and in April 1927 made a treaty with Hungary, after which he publicly espoused the cause of treaty revision in Hungary's favour. By this time France had made treaties with Czechoslovakia and Yugoslavia as well as with Poland. Thus central Europe and the Balkans became divided into the clients of Italy and the

clients of France. 'In the long run only co-operation between
Italy and Czechoslovakia could ensure Austria's survival.'[1]
Once this had broken down it would be easy for a resurgent
Germany to disturb the *status quo*. As the years went by
Mussolini more and more thought in terms of hampering
and tricking the democratic states, who on the whole supported the *status quo*, and encouraging anti-democratic movements or rulers. When General Primo de Rivera became
more or less dictator of Spain in 1923 Mussolini hoped for
great advantages which did not, however, materialise.

By 1927 the Italian Diplomatic Documents show
Mussolini's foreign policy to have become that of the chief
anti-democratic conspirator of Europe: the corollary of this
was that Fascist Italy, in becoming aggressively revisionist,
became more openly what she was bound to be, the enemy
of the League of Nations. The official visit of the Hungarian
Prime Minister, Count Bethlen, to Rome in April 1927 was
followed by arrangements for Italy to send arms to Hungary,
which was disarmed according to the Peace Treaties earlier
accepted by Mussolini. Thus the despatch of arms, anti-
quated though they were, from Italy to Hungary via
Austria, became an important Central European issue;
Austrian Socialists were able to denounce their passage
through Austria and this turned Mussolini's anger against
Socialism in Austria. It is worth noting, too, that later in
1927 Bethlen sent a Hungarian delegation to Rome to study
Fascism – just when the *Carta del Lavoro* had emerged but
five years too early for Mussolini's definition of his doctrine.
In 1927 also one finds demands for money coming to Musso-
lini from Austrian right-wing politicians, and visits to Rome
from the Croat separatists, Ivo Frank and Ante Pavelić.
Reports from Munich on Hitler did not impress Mussolini.

'As a journalist and ex-revolutionary, Mussolini was
fascinated by Lenin and the problem of Russia's future.'[2]
With the New Economic Policy he thought that Russia was
returning to capitalism; at all events he saw great com-

mercial possibilities for Italy if she came to terms with the U.S.S.R. For their part the Russians were eager to draw Italy into the Rapallo front with Germany. When on 30 November 1923 Mussolini announced that a commercial treaty with Russia would be accompanied by *de jure* recognition, Moscow newspapers welcomed this as the first 'breach in the old Entente united front against Soviet Russia'. Later when Gramsci* was arrested and sentenced and his colleague, Togliatti, remained as a Communist official in Moscow, relations between Italy and Russia nevertheless seemed undisturbed.

With Britain Mussolini's relationship was seldom unclouded. There was much feeling in Italy against both France and Britain because at the end of the war they had shared out the extra-European mandates without reference to Italy: it was thought that the omissions in carrying out the Treaty of London of April 1915 might have led to compensation for Italy in Africa, but in fact the mandates were distributed at the time when Orlando had left the Peace Conference. Over Corfu the French government under Poincaré had been more indulgent towards Italy than Britain in order to gain Italian support on the German question – the French occupation of the Ruhr in January 1923 had created great tension, not least between Paris and London. Mussolini, however, played his hand well. In November 1923 he placated the British by declaring his opposition to any further occupation of Germany. Curzon was trying to persuade Italy to cede at least part of the Dodecanese† against the African territory of Jubaland adjacent to Italian Somaliland. But after the Labour Government had come in, in July 1924 Jubaland was at last ceded to Italy without conditions. In December the Conservatives were back in power in Westminster and Austen Chamberlain

* See above, pp. 10, 20.
† Greek islands occupied by the Italians during the Libyan war and never evacuated.

went to Rome for the meeting of the Council of the League of Nations. Chamberlain made a point of consulting Mussolini who rejoiced at this seeming support from abroad at the end of the Matteotti year. So long as Chamberlain was in power he remained on friendly terms with Mussolini whom he seemed to like genuinely.

The thickest cloud over Anglo-Italian relations was Mussolini's resentment of the power of the British Navy. He particularly disliked the knowledge that the British fleet dominated 'Italy's sea', the Mediterranean, since the British were the masters of both Gibraltar and Suez. He had asserted himself against the Greeks, yet he did not rule even the Adriatic. Even the path to East Africa crossed the Mediterranean.

Towards the end of 1925 it became obvious that Mussolini's foreign policy was becoming more aggressive; writing in *Gerarchia* he even declared that 'the Fascist revolution will have its Napoleonic year in 1926'[3] and early in that year Contarini was forced out of office. At this time Mussolini created a crisis over South Tirol. Fascist policy was one of ruthless centralisation in any case and of ruthless denationalisation of Italy's German- or Slav-speaking minorities – *italianità* was to be physically imposed and impressed upon them. Just before Mussolini first took power in October 1922 *squadristi* had overrun Bolzano (Bozen), behaving with great brutality to the formerly Austrian population. The Fascist leader in this case was the fanatical Tolomei, who had, already before this, intimidated the German-speaking population in the name of the sanctity of the Brenner frontier. In the spring of 1923 Tolomei was made a Senator and given every encouragement to italianise without mercy. The Italian language was enforced in the law-courts and the schools and it became punishable to use German place-names even where Italian ones had to be invented. After a speech of protest in February 1926 from the Bavarian Prime Minister, Mussolini lashed himself into a fury. The Alto Adige, he declared, was 'geographically and historically Italian', and the Brenner frontier was 'a frontier traced by the infallible hand of God'; so far from lowering the Italian flag on the Brenner, 'Fascist Italy would if necessary carry it beyond'. Stresemann replied to this speech with some spirit, reminding Mussolini that the Brenner frontier had not been guaranteed at Locarno. But there was no way of protecting the South Tirolese because Italy ranked as a Great Power and could not be called to account by the League of Nations to abide by the Minorities Treaty drawn up by the League. Thus there was no way of seriously discouraging Mussolini whose attention was, however, diverted for the time being by a visit to Libya which excited his imperialistic hunger.

The policy of italianisation was cardinal to Fascism and the conception of the subjection of the individual to the state. It was not necessarily racial: that is to say no one was inevitably damned for what they happened to be born. One has the impression that over the South Tirol Mussolini was wildly emotional. Perhaps this in part went back to his time in Trent in 1909 and his expulsion by the Austrian authorities. His intransigence over this matter was to play into the hands of Hitler in two ways: (1) Hitler could always mollify Mussolini by offering to guarantee the Brenner frontier: he did this when he met Tolomei in 1928. (2) The Austrians already disliked the Italians; as the years passed the persecution of the Germans in South Tirol, so much worse than the treatment of any other German-speaking minority, made Austrian sentiment increasingly pro-Nazi, since Hitler, ironically enough, was felt by the Austrians to be the only remedy.

For the next twelve years, with the possible exception of the period of the Abyssinian war, the question of Austria can never have been far from Mussolini's mind. Austria was necessarily the connecting link with Hungary. Economically, owing to its iron and its timber as well as its tourist attractions, Austria was never permanently in danger, but politically from the time of the burning down of the law-courts in 1927 its condition began to become precarious. According to an Austrian right-wing leader, Prince Starhemberg himself, he first met Mussolini in 1930 who insisted to him that an Anschluss with Germany could never be permitted. This was one reason why in November 1930 Mussolini subsidised the Austrian *Heimwehr* against the Austrian Nazis in the Austrian elections. In the spring of 1931 the abortive plan for an Austro-German Customs Union helped to bring about the collapse of the *Creditanstalt* in Vienna. Already in September 1930 the Nazis had gained 107 seats in the German Reichstag.

In analysing Fascism in Italy one is concerned only with its own operation at home and abroad; in analysing its influence, German National Socialism will be dealt with later on and Austria as well. Fascist foreign policy was debilitated at this stage by a lack of comprehension on Mussolini's part. Tamaro[4] says that in the earlier thirties he really thought the Austrians were distinct from the Germans; on the other hand he probably never grasped how funda-mentally Austrian and *Grossdeutsch* Hitler was. This meant that Hitler's first aim was to absorb Austria into Germany and that he pursued the traditional *Mitteleuropa* policy which Professor Fritz Fischer has shown to have dominated the German government's mind, as well as that of Austria and Hungary, already during the First World War.

Naturally Mussolini had followed the fortunes of Adolf Hitler with interest. At first he was unable to take him seriously and there is no reason to suppose that he ever financed the German National Socialists. During 1932 he expected Hitler to sweep to power, but in November when the Nazis lost two million votes, like many others Mussolini thought they had missed their chance. However, it was delightfully flattering when his seeming disciple was ap-pointed Chancellor of Germany in January 1933. The idea

1*a*. Giovanni Giolitti

1*b*. Benedetto Croce

1*c*. Giacomo Matteotti

1*d*. Giovanni Gentile

2*a*. Italo Balbo

2*b*. Count Dino Grandi prepares to
present his credentials, London 1932

3*a*. Gabriele d'Annunzio

3*b*. Roberto Farinacci, 1940

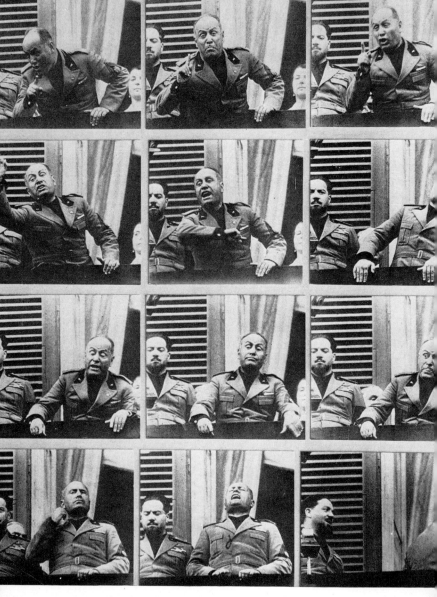

4 *and* 5*a, b, c.* The Duce's public face—Balbo is with him above

6a. *top left:* Young Fascists march past Mussolini on the outbreak of the Abyssinian War, October 1935

6b. *bottom left:* Mussolini with Badoglio

7a. *right:* Mussolini with King Victor Emmanuel

7b. *below:* Mussolini signs the Lateran Pact

8a. Ciano with Kanya and Schuschnigg in Vienna, 1936

8b. Mussolini with Hitler in Germany, September 1937

that Fascism was the conquering creed of the twentieth century seemed to be reinforced. But two disagreeable consequences followed almost immediately: Nazi agitation in Austria against the Christian-Social Chancellor Dollfuss was intensified and Hitler announced a boycott of Jewish shops in Germany for 1 April. This anti-Semitism, Mussolini felt, would discredit the dictatorships, and he instructed his Ambassador in Berlin to convey his opinion to Hitler: the Führer, however, in spite of his apparent reverence for Mussolini, declared in so many words that the Duce did not know what he was talking about.

At about the time that Hitler came to power Mussolini spoke to Starhemberg[5] of the Danubian basin as 'our European hinterland'. He felt that immediate action was required as Hitler would waste no time about rearming. If Starhemberg is to be relied on, Mussolini suggested some kind of union between Austria, Hungary and Croatia (thus by now assuming the disintegration of Yugoslavia) with Italian economic backing. The upshot a little later was the Rome Protocols of March 1934 to promote trade between only Italy, Austria and Hungary. Meanwhile in June 1933 Mussolini had launched the venture of the Four-Power Pact, which attempted to break up existing alignments by creating a special relationship between the Great Powers of France, Britain, Germany and Italy. It disturbed France's small-power allies and aimed at assuaging Germany's appetite by emphasising her Great-Power status without allowing her to swallow Austria. Hitler, however, spoilt this pattern by quarrelling with, and leaving, the League of Nations in October 1933.

Just after his Four-Power Pact Mussolini made a fatal error. He wrote to Dollfuss pressing him to act against the Austrian Social Democrats – Mussolini had his own grievance against them over the 'Hirtenberg Affair', as it was called, when in January 1933 they had again exposed him as sending arms to Hungary via the Hirtenberg armaments

C

factory in Austria. He also supposed that the Nazis would cash in with their anti-Marxist propaganda if the Austrian Socialists were left undisturbed. There is little doubt that pressure from Rome helped to bring about the four-day civil war in Austria in February 1934 in which the Socialists were destroyed. The result was that many a Viennese workman joined the clandestine Austrian Nazis in desperation against the clerical pressure countenanced by the Austrian government.

Meanwhile the old idea of revenge on Abyssinia for the defeat of Adowa in 1896 fitted in very well with imperial notions and Roman ambitions, although Abyssinia was never part of the Roman Empire. It has been seen that Mussolini was trying to send up the Italian birth-rate, and although, as we have seen, he sometimes disclaimed this, he thirsted for expansion in terms of territory too. From the summer of 1934 onwards it seems that the Duce was preparing for some kind of clash with the Ethiopians. To conquer them was undoubtedly dictated by *Fascismo*; the timing of the operation, however, depended upon the state of the Italian armed forces and the situation in Europe. Although the Duce's 'Doctrine' should have prepared the Italians for war by now, and the Wal Wal incident* conveniently occurred in December 1934, preparations were inadequate until the second half of 1935. The rearmament of Germany – conscription announced in March 1935 – and Hitler's designs upon Austria indicated an Italian attack on Abyssinia in the autumn of 1935. Then by the spring of 1936 the Italian armed forces, the Duce thought, could be back in Europe to curb Hitler if necessary and to guard the Danube basin.

Before the Abyssinian war, in the summer of 1934, Mussolini was to have new experiences of Hitlerism for

---

* This was a military clash between Italians and Ethiopians in an area where the frontier between Italian Somaliland and Ethiopia had not been definitively drawn.

which he was not prepared. In the middle of June in Stra and Venice he had his first encounters with Hitler when the two dictators talked past one another. At the end of June Hitler massacred some eighty Germans whose existence irked him, including his old friend, S.A. chief Ernst Röhm, and also General Schleicher. The murder of Matteotti alone had caused so much more commotion in Italy that Mussolini was certainly disagreeably surprised. Finally at the end of July Dollfuss, whose wife was Mussolini's guest at the time, was murdered by Austrian S.S. men, Hitler only disclaiming a connection when it was found that Dollfuss's Cabinet colleagues were able to keep the Austrian government in their hands. If *Fascismo* meant well-timed violence, National Socialism seemed rather to spell violence wholesale, in addition to barbarous racial notions. The compliment of Hitler's deference to Mussolini was indeed doubtful. At Bari on 6 September 1934, speaking from a tank at the fifth *Fiera del Levante*, Mussolini declared: 'Thirty centuries of history allow us to regard with supreme indulgence certain doctrines taught beyond the Alps by the descendants of people who were wholly illiterate in the days when Caesar, Virgil and Augustus flourished in Rome.' Already in 1934, before Hitler reintroduced conscription, the Duce was thinking in terms of a quick grab in Africa to forestall Hitler should he hit out beyond Germany's existing frontiers.

Early in January 1935, when the French Prime Minister Laval went to Rome, Mussolini decided that it was worth his while to abandon Italy's privileges in Tunisia in order to have what really came to French approval of the defence of Austria and of undefined Italian action in Ethiopia.[6] The agreement with Laval seemed a very un-Fascist performance; it was certainly anti-German in spite of the rule of his disciple over Germany. It occasioned comments from Italian Foreign Office officials on Mussolini's basic preference for France, 1789 and Third Republic and all. The agreement with France of January 1935 was followed by the

Stresa conference when Britain joined France and Italy in April. The final declaration at Stresa was as follows:

The three Powers, the objective of whose policy is the collective maintenance of peace within the framework of the League of Nations, find themselves in complete agreement in opposing, by all practical means, any unilateral repudiation of treaties which may endanger the peace of Europe, and will act in close and cordial collaboration for this purpose.

The words 'of Europe' were inserted by Mussolini himself after consulting the members of the conference; the British, represented by Simon, MacDonald and Vansittart, made no objection whatever for they remained silent. After this the Italian press became violently anti-British while remaining friendly to France. Within a year Mussolini had conquered Ethiopia. The objections of the League of Nations expressed by Eden of Britain had given the Abyssinian war great popularity in Italy.* Fascist propaganda against the British, who, it was claimed, had in the past grabbed what they wanted and now blocked Italy, was effective. The Church supported the Italian government. The fact that slavery continued in Ethiopia gave the Italians a moral mission in regard to its conquest. When Mussolini in May 1936 made Victor Emmanuel into Emperor of Abyssinia the Italians as a whole were as enthusiastic about the Fascist régime as they ever had been, possibly more so, for Fascism seemed really to have served Italy.

But Mussolini had conquered Ethiopia at the cost of defiance of the League of Nations, at the cost of a rift with France and especially with Britain, but also at the cost of a rift between the two Western Powers. This emasculated the League and gave Hitler encouragement to remilitarise the Rhineland. What did Fascist foreign policy dictate now?

* As the Hoare–Laval Plan was abortive, it seems irrelevant to discuss it here. There will be a separate volume in this series entitled *Mussolini, Abyssinia and the League.*

Inexorably it condemned the West as possessive and decadent, the League as pacifist and liberal. Inexorably, too, it gravitated towards the support of the greatest protagonist of violence and tyranny the world has known, Adolf Hitler. In becoming a satellite of Nazi Germany, Fascist Italy would destroy itself. Was this because the corporative system had never really worked, because the *Gioventù Italiana del Littorio* had failed to make young Italy love war?

The mirage of the Spanish Civil War intervened in July 1936; this replaced the mirage of Austria for Mussolini. For at some point in 1936 he recognised that Italy was extremely unpopular in Austria and that Italian support discredited the Austrian government: hence he countenanced the Austro-German Agreement in July which destroyed real Austrian independence. But just at this time a military rising in Spain, whose leaders appealed to him for help against an ultra-liberal government, was fascinating. Again he felt confirmed in the belief that the creed he had invented was the century's conquering creed. Italy agreed to help Franco far more generously and more imprudently* than Hitler, who until nearly the end only sent *Luftwaffe* contingents to acquire some practical experience. Mussolini, on the other hand, sent large contingents of infantry. He expected to become a kind of Lord Protector of Spain and possibly to annex a Spanish island or so. By the spring of 1939, when the Spanish Civil War at last brought victory to Franco, Fascist Italy had been gravely impoverished and in part humiliated by, for instance, the battle of Guadalajara in 1937. On that occasion the Italian Fascist troops were harried by Italian anti-Fascist soldiers, including Mussolini's old Republican friend, Pietro Nenni, who had volunteered to fight for the Spanish Republic – Mussolini was always hyper-sensitive about the activities of the anti-Fascists unless

* 70,000 Italian troops had been sent by 1937, according to Kirkpatrick: *Mussolini: Study of a Demagogue*. There will be a separate volume in this series entitled *The European Powers and the Spanish Civil War*.

he could ridicule them successfully. It is interesting that Tamaro admits that Guadalajara had an adverse effect upon Italian opinion.

As for Italian influence over Franco's Spain it turned out to be minimal.* In the meantime the Italian soldiers had made themselves very unpopular.

* See below, p. 116.

[1] C. Seton-Watson, *Italy from Liberalism to Fascism*, p. 682.
[2] Ibid., p. 683.
[3] Ibid., p. 697.
[4] Tamaro, *Vent'anni di Storia*.
[5] E. R. von Starhemberg, *Between Hitler and Mussolini* (1942).
[6] See *D.D.F.*, series II, vol. I.

5 Decline Sets in at Home and Abroad

SOME writers have held that Mussolini's appointment of his son-in-law, Galeazzo Ciano, to be Foreign Minister in June 1936 marked a stage in the decline, indeed perhaps the first stage in the disintegration, of Fascism in Italy. It certainly marked a stage in *Mussolinismo*, for the Duce expected to be blindly obeyed by young Ciano. It marks a stage for historians because from 1937 onwards Ciano's Diaries recorded Mussolini's thoughts, probably faithfully. Fascism now tended to consist of the vacillations of a man of declining health who suffered from a duodenal ulcer, a man to whom no one now cared to tell the truth. The man himself was becoming disillusioned. He began to realise that he had not transformed the Italians into a nation of warriors. He knew that, perhaps even before the general recognition of Abyssinia as Italian, his personal popularity was beginning to fade. It has been seen that he preferred to abuse what he chose to call the *borghesia*, but there is little reason to suppose that Mussolini was more popular with the Italian working classes, rather the contrary. He had always gone in for affairs with women in a way which was repellent rather than attractive, but they had been kept in the background. In 1936 he established Clara Petacci as his reigning mistress with a room in the Palazzo Venezia where he worked; the intrigues of her relatives, who were connected with the Black or Papal aristocracy, added to the unpopularity of this arrangement on the part of a man who, since 1929, had, after all, found it expedient to express respect for the life of the family, whatever went on in the Fascist Party. Now, through the Petaccis, corruption crept closer to him. In a way Ciano helped this tendency, though he disliked the Petaccis. Although since the last days of Matteotti, corruption in the Fascist Party had been constantly revealed, Mussolini himself had never allowed his reputation to be soiled by this. He was modest in his personal tastes as well as being a man who worked very hard and could not be reproached with making much of the spoils of office. Galeazzo Ciano was just the opposite and, into the bargain, indiscreet about his entanglements.

After Ciano's appointment as Foreign Minister, when he returned from fighting in Abyssinia, it was observed that the other two men now closest to Mussolini were the chief of the police, Arturo Bocchini, and a new figure called Guido Buffarini-Guidi, originally a protégé of the elder Ciano: Buffarini-Guidi became Under-Secretary in the Ministry of the Interior towards the end of 1933. From here he took care to try to please the powerful Bocchini; he also intrigued with the Petacci family, procuring favours particularly for Clara Petacci's brother, Marcello. Among other changes of personnel in 1936 it is worth noting that Suvich was sent as Italian Ambassador to Washington while Bastianini succeeded him as Under-Secretary at the Foreign Office. De Vecchi, who had been Minister of National Education, was sent in spite of his hatred for the Greeks to govern the Dodecanese,[1] when Bottai, it has been seen, stepped into his place.

In June 1937 there occurred the typically Fascist creation of a *Ministero della Cultura Popolare* or Ministry of Popular Culture, which was soon known by the ridiculing abbreviation of the 'Minculpop'. Essentially an imitation of Goebbels's 'Ministry for the Enlightenment of the People and Propaganda', which went back to 1933, the 'Minculpop' was an extension of the Ministry for the Press and Propaganda where Dino Alfieri had succeeded Ciano; Alfieri now became head of the 'Minculpop'. He was no longer merely to control the press and emasculate the news, but rather to make Fascist the whole culture and spirit of the Italian people by supervising books, theatre, cinema, broadcasting. In order not to waste their time and money, publishers and authors now nearly all submitted their products for the approval of the 'Minculpop'. Only the Ministry of Education attempted to defend itself against the 'Minculpop's' claims, and Bottai was on the whole a stouter man than Alfieri. In the last instance the Duce would decide. It was he personally who urged the celebration, in September 1937, of two thousand years having passed since Augustus became Emperor, with an exhibition of Roman things; at the same time there was an exhibition of the Fascist Revolution.[1]

The Fascist régime was always rather worried by the country's intellectuals for fear that they should use their reason; they were constantly exhorted by the representatives of Fascism to have faith rather than to think. As late as February 1939 Giuseppe Prezzolini, Mussolini's old supporter from the days of *La Voce* in Florence, conveniently maintained in an article that he wrote that 'The place of the intelligence in life is limited and subsidiary.' In 1937 the well-known writer Papini was made a member of the Academy of Italy – this was suitable enough but it was exceptional that so gifted a man should receive this honour. A little later d'Annunzio was made its President, but by now he was seventy-five and within a few months of his death on 1 March 1938.

The only liberal publications, apart from Croce's, which were now unlikely to be interfered with, were translations of foreign books: curiously, quite a number of these, of a quite un-Fascist nature, were permitted by the Duce for a few more years.

From 1936 until the end nothing can be discerned that deserves the name of Italian foreign policy, nothing but a surrender to the pressure from Hitler with no regard for Italy's interest or capacity. In October 1936 Ciano was sent to Berlin to sign the October Protocols by which Italy gained nothing but phrases about collaboration against Communism.

On 1 November Mussolini made a speech at Milan in which he referred to a Berlin–Rome line which was 'not a diaphragm but rather an axis around which can revolve all those European states with a will to collaboration and peace'. This meant that he was allowing Hitler into his 'European hinterland'. Within less than a year Mussolini had accepted an invitation to visit Germany whose power henceforth fascinated him to an extent which proved paralysing.

In the place of any foreign policy there occurred a number of inconsistent definitions of Fascism which comprised an integral part of the later history of Fascism in Italy. One significant feature of Mussolini's visit to Germany by Hitler's special invitation in September 1937 was a condition the Duce attached to his acceptance: he said that he wished to be allowed to address the German masses in German. This attempt to communicate with a different nation seemed to express the ambition to make Italian Fascism expand into Germany as the country of the 'sister revolution', and thence no doubt beyond. His speech in Berlin on the Maifeld, overtaken by torrents of rain, was, however, a dismal failure.

This visit to Germany was, nevertheless, of the greatest importance. Hitherto Mussolini had not overcome the dislike and contempt he had felt towards Germany and the Germans all his life, or certainly since his time in Trent in 1909. His only earlier meeting with Hitler in June 1934 had not altered this. But now the Führer had become a much more impressive figure politically, a man who had successfully defied the Europe of Versailles. Moreover, Hitler and his myrmidons set out to display all their strength. They set out to emphasise an intimate relationship between the National Socialist and the Fascist revolutions and to flatter Mussolini as the pioneer of both. They arranged to show Mussolini their army manœuvres at Mecklenburg and how armaments were manufactured by Krupp at Essen. There is little doubt that the impressionable Mussolini was, as it were, swept off his feet. He had reviewed countless parades of soldiers in connection with the Ethiopian war and the Civil War in Spain now entering its second year, but the Germans' display certainly outshone all that he had seen at home. Mussolini henceforth believed with as much consistency as he could summon up that he must link the fate of Italy and himself to the Nazi stronghold of power, and share the spoils of a shared defeat of decadent France and Britain. It should be added that in the previous June Mussolini had again been associated with political murder when French *cagoulards* at the instance of subordinates of Ciano had murdered in France the hero of the Savona trial, the outstanding anti-Fascist, Carlo Rosselli. Rosselli had broadcast in France a message which exasperated Mussolini; it began 'Today in Spain, tomorrow in Italy. . . .' The murder was made possible by Fascist intrigues with anti-Republican groupings in France. To this extent Italian Fascism was international.

As Salvatorelli and Mira point out, the Italian government, though basically lacking the conviction of its earlier days, became in all directions more aggressive now. The young Ciano gloried in this and made a point of protruding his chin in the manner of his father-in-law making some bellicose statement. Early in 1938 a change was introduced in everyday life which annoyed the Italian public. They were told to address each other, apart from the more intimate *tu*, as *voi* instead of *Lei*, because *Lei* was decadent, undignified, middle-class, un-Fascist. It is characteristic of this period of Fascism that something so trivial should have occupied the attention of the authorities. The ordinary Italian felt that he was being ordered to be discourteous, apart, that is, from the Neapolitans who had used *voi* before. Indeed Croce now carefully changed his habits and proceeded to use *Lei* instead of *voi*. At the same time Mussolini tried to prevent the Italians from shaking hands, for he wished them to salute each other only in the Roman fashion. On 1 February 1938 the goose-step from Germany was introduced into the Italian Army; it was, however, called the 'passo romano' and the newspapers described it as 'strong, secure, inexorable . . . making every march into a conquest'. Mussolini displayed petulant anger every time it was suggested that he was making the Italians imitate the Germans. These more or less futile novelties caused the smouldering dislike between the Duce and the King to rekindle a small flame, for the latter always resented interference with the Army, particularly of the kind the goose-step implied. Victor Emmanuel never cared for Mussolini's *rapprochement* with Nazi Germany.

When the Anschluss came in March 1938* Mussolini tried to make the best of it by ready acceptance. But it was clear to the Italian public, in spite of the 'Minculpop', that Mussolini had been humiliated by Hitler, and with this Italy's position in Europe had become more precarious. At the end of March Ciano *père* proposed in the Chamber, over which he presided, that a new rank should be created, Marshal of the Empire, and that it should be conferred on the King and the Duce. This was carried by acclamation (the Fascist way of voting now) in both Chamber and Senate. The King openly objected this time on behalf of the constitutional position of the Army. But then he withdrew, leaving Mussolini – and Starace – grumbling over the Monarchy. Early in May Hitler with an enormous suite visited Italy. Besides emphasising the virility of the Axis alliance this sharpened the tension between the Crown and the Duce; the German visitors made it clear that they regarded the Monarchy as superfluous, and Mussolini constantly felt resentment that the King according to protocol was paired off with Hitler, while the Duce had to take a back-seat if the King was present. There was mutual dislike between Victor Emmanuel and Hitler.

It was in 1938 that Mussolini for the first time incorporated

* See, in this series, Christopher Thorne, *The Approach of War, 1938–1939* (1967).

anti-Semitism as a part of Fascist doctrine. Less than anywhere in Europe was any anti-Semitic feeling to be found in Italy: it is true to say that there was no problem at all. In the early days of Fascism, when all sorts of fantastic extremisms were being aired, occasionally an anti-Semitic phrase had been heard, particularly in Trieste where big business was Jewish and sometimes nostalgic about the Habsburg past. But this was exceptional. An anti-Semitic paper called *Il Tevere* had existed in Rome for years. It was said to be financed by Nazi Germans and was not taken at all seriously. There was a certain hostility among Italian Fascists towards Zionism[2] precisely because the Italian Jews were regarded as Italians: they were a very small minority but an honoured one. Although a Jew like Carlo Rosselli had been an anti-Fascist leader and a good many Jews had been freemasons, other Jews had supported Fascism. For years Mussolini had taken the line that it would be as fatal to quarrel with the Jews as with the Catholic Church, and it has been seen that in the spring of 1933 he had tried to dissuade Hitler from anti-Jewish measures. Fascism had been defined as nothing to do with race.

By 1936 Mussolini began to show signs of a change. For one thing the Ethiopian war made him more aware of questions concerning relations between races of different colour. For another he was increasingly eager to win the support of the Arab world. There can be no doubt, however, that the chief cause was the Rome–Berlin Axis. The more Fascist Italy was associated with Nazi Germany the more it tended to appear as anti-Semitic and the more it courted the enmity of Jews the world over. Fascist Italy had, however, made little difficulty in allowing German Jews to take refuge within her frontiers. Occasionally these tragically disgruntled exiles created personal friction on a tiny scale – it is well known that the German Jews were often tactless, but they again comprised no serious problem. In actual fact, although Mussolini always denied it as absurd when it was said that he was imitating Hitler, this is precisely what he ended up by doing almost with servility.

It was in September 1936, exactly one year before the Duce's visit to Germany, that Farinacci began an anti-Semitic campaign in his newspaper, the *Regime Fascista* of Cremona. When Hans Frank (in September 1936) or Ribbentrop (in November 1937) visited him, Mussolini half boasted of this. Farinacci was befriended by a renegade priest called Giovanni Preziosi, who had long directed an anti-Semitic review called *Vita Italiana* but had hitherto been regarded as a freak. Farinacci was another matter, an early Fascist leader and a member of the Fascist Grand Council: ominously in June 1938 he was made a Minister of State. Nevertheless as late as February 1938 the Italian Foreign Office, whose head was Ciano, declared that 'a specific Jewish question does not exist in Italy', adding faintly disturbing qualifications.[3]

There is no evidence that Hitler ever exerted any direct pressure on Mussolini about the Italian Jews: the subject is not known to have been mentioned between them. But his visit to Italy in May 1938 seemed to set the seal upon the mastery he had gained over Mussolini in the previous September. Thanks to the personal fascination which he henceforth inspired in the Duce, Fascism in Italy lost its character and became a poor, half-hearted imitation of German National Socialism. It should not be forgotten that Hitler's fascination for Mussolini was nourished by the almost exalted admiration which the Führer expressed for the Duce. Hitler's very visit, incidentally, had induced anti-Jewish police measures because the Italian police had had orders to round up any Jew living near the official routes that would be taken by the Nazi leaders.

It was not until a few months later that Mussolini introduced anti-Semitic legislation. It was presented as a continuation of the Duce's much-vaunted demographic policy. This had hitherto rested on the simple assumption that numbers give strength and the tacit implication that an overpopulated country can be excused for expanding into someone else's territory. To the care and help which had so far been handed out to pregnant women and particularly to the mothers of large families, to the cult of personal fitness in the para-military youth formations, there must now in 1938 be added consideration for the fitness of the Italian race (whatever that might be). The Italian race must in future not be corrupted by racial mixture. And in this context the Italian Jews were suddenly branded as not Italian at all. Under the aegis, it was said, of the 'Minculpop', ten scientists defined 'the position of Fascism with regard to the problems of race', and this was the upshot. One needs to have read Natalia Ginzburg's *Lessico familiare* to understand the sudden shock experienced by her family, the gifted Levis of Turin, and their friends, when for no other reason her father, who was an able scientist, no longer young, was suddenly dismissed from his position in the university. In so far as Mussolini was not merely dragged along in Hitler's wake he probably felt that Fascism had lost its *élan* and that a coercive novelty might help to renew it. But there can be little doubt that the Italians as a nation condemned anti-Semitism, and felt humiliated by, as they saw it, already becoming a German satellite. Many of them had been proud since 1933 that Fascism was not racially intolerant like Nazi Germany. The Pope had condemned 'exaggerated nationalism' in any case and many Italian Catholics had been thankful that Mussolini had not imposed the racial heresy upon them. Even most of the leading Fascists were privately displeased by the introduction of anti-Semitism.

In April 1938 the Council of Ministers had approved the establishment of an Institute in Rome for 'la bonifica umana e l'ortogenesi',* and soon Starace was goading on the Institute of Fascist Culture, the G.U.F. and the Fascist women's organisations to study the characteristics of the

* Human reconditioning and eugenics.

Italian race. He discovered that anti-Semitism was anti-bourgeois. On 1 September a decree proposed by Mussolini forbade all foreign Jews to settle anywhere on Italian territory in Europe or Africa. On 2 September, according to a proposal from the formerly critical Minister of Education Bottai, Jews were forbidden to teach in all state schools and expelled from all academic bodies. Finally by the racial law of 10 November Jews were expelled from all state jobs, from the Party, from the corporations, from banking and insurance, but with exceptions made in the case of holders of war decorations or special services to Fascism.[4] Jews, however, were defined as persons both of whose parents had been Jewish, not as in Germany where one Jewish grandparent condemned the victims of Hitler's persecution. Even so the nature of Fascism was perverted, for hitherto it had never condemned anyone solely for the accident of their birth: Germans or Slavs in Italy could become Italianised, if they were willing to be, and thereby wholly acceptable.

At this time Mussolini wished not only to stir up feeling against the Jews but also against France, 'to free the Italians from their last servitude, their attitude towards Paris'. He told Ciano he wanted to make the Italians nastier, more Prussian, 'hard, implacable, hateful, in other words masters'.[5] His intolerance towards King and Pope was rekindled. He came out with, from Italy's point of view, a quite superfluous enthusiasm in support of Hitler's attitude towards Czechoslovakia, making aggressive speeches on the subject at Trieste, Treviso, Padua in September, the last in the series at Verona on 26 September: these warlike speeches were received with applause. It is difficult to suppose that the Duce's outbursts inclined Chamberlain to appeal to Mussolini to propose to Hitler a conference between Germany, Italy, France and Britain instead of a German invasion of Czechoslovakia. The Munich Conference and the Agreement to which it led in the short run brought popularity to the four leaders involved because the thought of war was generally hateful. Above all Mussolini was praised for his contribution; his initiative in proposing the conference together with his relative linguistic ability made him the central figure at Munich, and his personal popularity soared back briefly to the level of May 1936.

A technique typical of Fascism almost more than it was of National Socialism was now adopted by Mussolini and Ciano – it was not new but reached new heights. On 30 November 1938 Ciano made a speech in the Chamber, speaking of Italy's national aspirations. The deputies very conveniently began to shout 'Tunis, Djibouti, Corsica!', or, according to Ciano's Diary, 'Tunis, Corsica, Nice and Savoy'. Such cries were insulting to France, but the Fascist authorities did nothing to still them, rather the reverse. At the same time Mussolini chose to be rude to the new French Ambassador, André François-Poncet, who had ironically enough been transferred from Berlin to Rome because in Paris they thought that Hitler was influenced by Mussolini.

The year 1939 was a Fascist climax. At last, in February of that year, as we have seen above, the *Carta della Scuola* was completed and came into force, integrating at least in theory all the machinery of Fascist education. Just before this the skeleton of the former Italian Parliament had been given new flesh. The Chamber would in future be substituted by the meeting together of the National Council of the Fascist Party (about 150 members), the National Council of the Corporations (about 500 members) and the Fascist Grand Council, between 650 and 700 people altogether and all Mussolini's nominees. The speech from the throne held on one of the special Fascist anniversaries, 23 March, that of the meeting at Piazza San Sepolcro in March 1919, put much emphasis upon the Fascist policy of economic self-sufficiency or autarchy. At about the same time the last academic institution which had retained a certain independence, the *Accademia dei Lincei*, was amalgamated with the Fascist

Accademia d'Italia. Almost simultaneously various books by
Russians, such as Gogol, Tolstoy, Turgenev and by Jews,
were withdrawn from circulation.[6] Thus Italy's culture
became more narrowly Fascist and the foreign translations
became restricted.

The completion of the Fascist totalitarian state required
an aggressive foreign policy with the risk of war. In
November 1937 Italy had adhered to the anti-Comintern
Pact first signed between Germany and Japan the year
before. In addition to provocative taunting of the French,
Ciano had planned for some time an Italian seizure of
Albania to replace the Italian protection of that country
since 1926. Unfortunately for Mussolini Hitler seized Prague
in the middle of March 1939, thereby acquiring a key
position from the strategic, as from the economic, point of
view. When, three weeks later, the Italians chose Good
Friday to invade Albania it looked like a childish gesture of
assertion in reply to the Ally, Hitler: the chosen day was not
likely to appeal to Catholic opinion. Albania was thus
annexed and Victor Emmanuel became its king.

The story of the Nazi–Fascist Steel Pact has been told
often enough by now. When Hitler came to Italy in May
1938, Ribbentrop offered the Italians a military alliance;
they refused on the grounds that Italian public opinion was
not ripe for it. Early in May 1939 Ciano and Ribbentrop
met in Milan, Ciano with instructions from Mussolini to
make an alliance with the Germans now, provided that war
was not risked until after 1942 when the Duce planned to
hold an international exhibition in Rome in order to bring
in precious foreign currency. Ribbentrop was pleasantly
surprised, and agreed by word of mouth to the delay. During
the evening of 6 May Ciano telephoned to his father-in-law
in Rome to report German acquiescence. Now Mussolini
was at this time over-excited by journalistic quips in the
French press about anti-German feeling in Milan; he was
also anxious over references in the House of Commons the

day before to Anglo-Turkish negotiations. When Ciano rang up he ordered him immediately to make a public announcement that a written Italo-German alliance had been agreed upon. This impulsive command made it possible for the Germans to dictate terms. They put forward a pact which proposed aggressive collusion – as Mussolini said at one point, no one intended to attack the Axis Powers so that a defensive treaty would have been pointless. Article III of the Treaty, which came to be called the Steel Pact, stated: 'If it should happen, against the wishes and hopes of the contracting parties, that one of them becomes involved in warlike complications with another Power or with other Powers, the other contracting party will come to its aid as an ally and will support it with all its military forces on land, on sea and in the air.' The futility of Fascist diplomacy was completed by rushing into these obligations as drafted by the Germans with no written safeguards as to the delay for which the Italians had asked. 'In point of fact by this treaty Mussolini gave him [Hitler] *carte blanche* to attack Poland and to plunge into the Second World War.'[7]

[1] Salvatorelli and Mira, *Storia d'Italia*, pp. 898–9.
[2] R. De Felice, *Storia degli ebrei italiani sotto il fascismo.*
[3] Salvatorelli and Mira, op. cit., p. 980.
[4] Ibid., p. 993.
[5] See *Ciano's Diaries.*
[6] Salvatorelli and Mira, op. cit., p. 996.
[7] Wiskemann, *The Rome–Berlin Axis*, p. 181.

6 War and Downfall

IT has been indicated to how great an extent the Italians had been repelled by Fascism since it had become anti-Semitic and altogether a poor imitation of German National Socialism. The experience of the war in Ethiopia and the fighting in Spain had not made most Italians more bellicose. The more remarkable thing, however, about Mussolini's Fascism in 1939 was rather Italy's lack of armaments than her lack of fighting spirit. The Abyssinian and the Spanish campaigns had used up large stocks of military material, but things were much worse than they need have been because Fascism in practice had proved inefficient and, particularly in Ethiopia, corrupt, and no one cared to inform the Duce of the true state of things although he was often the Minister responsible. Only the Italian Navy, which impressed Hitler and his naval advisers in May 1938 as potentially useful to Germany, was in any condition to enter a war. People other than Mussolini knew this – the lack of military preparation was freely discussed. When Albania was seized it was an open secret that the operation went badly. If Fascism had reduced Italy to these straits what could justify it? When Hitler, without consulting Italy as the Steel Pact would seem to have required, attacked Poland on 1 September 1939 Mussolini had had to confess to him that without enormous supplies of raw materials from Germany Italy could not join in. It has been said that the autumn of 1939 saw the death of Fascism. Indeed it has been pointed out that King Victor Emmanuel would have been wiser to dismiss Mussolini then rather than waiting for nearly four years longer.

Between the autumn of 1939 and the fall of Mussolini

Fascism lost ground almost steadily. At first great relief was felt over the declaration of Italy's non-belligerency and there was sympathy with Poland and then Finland. But in the spring of 1940 it became clear that Italian intervention was coming. When it came many Italians were embarrassed by this apparent rushing in to seize spoils from a collapsing France, for it was true that Mussolini had not succeeded in destroying Italian sympathy with France, particularly not in June 1940.

Belligerency more than ever made Fascist Italy into Nazi Germany's vassal. German police and economic officials were established in Italy to supervise the Italian performance. After the disastrous Italian attack upon Greece – an easy prey, Mussolini thought – at the end of October 1940, the whole Italian operation had to be rescued by Hitler in the spring of 1941. Then he struck Yugoslavia down and broke Greek resistance, and shared the occupation of both countries with Mussolini. However, Italian protection – together with Germany's – over the Croatia of Pavelić, and the Italian acquisition at last of part of Dalmatia in 1941, came in circumstances which robbed them of popularity. Italy did now acquire (for about three years) the Dalmatian coast from north of Zara (Zadar) to south of Spalato (Split), and a considerable area around Cattaro (Kotor) together with most of the adjacent islands. Zara, which had itself belonged to Italy since 1919, was made the capital of the new Italian province which the Fascists called *la Dalmazia Storica*. Between August 1939 and June 1941 Mussolini also had the bitter experience of competing with Stalin for Hitler's friendship. After all he had said about Fascism's fight against Communism at home, abroad, and specially in Spain, he was further discredited in Italian eyes by being exposed as, via Hitler, Stalin's confederate. When the Tripartite Pact was signed in Berlin in September 1940 by Germany, Italy and Japan, the latter insisted that it should not be regarded as directed against Russia.

Two major blows to the Fascist state were war with the United States in December 1941, and in 1942 and 1943 the loss of the Italian Empire in Africa, together with Tunisia and Corsica, which had been temporarily acquired. The number of Italians who had emigrated to the United States was high, and to be at war with them was most painful. And then, after all that Fascism had said about Italian imperialism, not only Ethiopia and Tunisia were lost to the Allies, but also the pre-Fascist colonies of Libya and Eritrea were lost and lost for good. After the war Italy was given the United Nations trusteeship in her former colony, Somalia, for a limited period.

Bitter quarrels ensued with Nazi Germany over many issues. Franco refused to join the Axis though Mussolini had always treated him as an ideological, as well as a political, vassal, and the Axis failed to take Gibraltar in consequence: the Führer held the Duce responsible for this for the rest of his days. For some time Hitler seemed inclined to protect Pétain's France from Italian claims which were in fact never realised. In Yugoslavia there was something like a direct clash between Italian and German policy since the Italians used the Serbian Četnici to fight Tito's Partisans. Hitler said the Četnici as much as Tito's men must be annihilated, for he knew that all Serbs were bandits as they had appeared to him, Hitler, in Vienna before 1913.

Fascism now began to mean to Italians yet another form of subjection to Germany: Italian labour was increasingly sent to work in German factories among other foreign workers treated more or less as slaves. The Italians were sometimes maltreated by Nazi managers who did not show reverence for the Axis connection, but rather contempt for 'inferior' Latins.

Over Russia Mussolini possessed a basic flexibility alien to Hitler: it is interesting that the war against the U.S.S.R. was relatively young when the Duce began in his now feeble way to urge Hitler to come to terms with Moscow – Mussolini often pressed for this, though he never spoke of an accommodation with the West. Typically of the schizophrene he had become, it was he, not the other master-spirit, who insisted on Italian contingents being sent to the Russian front. There in the winter of Stalingrad 1942-3 they suffered terrible casualties. Already in November 1942 the Allies had landed in French North Africa.

In 1942 Italian morale obviously broke down from a Fascist point of view. Food became short, hostile air-raids became serious, 'everyone', it was said, listened to the B.B.C. Draconic sentences were pronounced upon people who had tried to exploit food shortages. Various Fascist officials were expelled from the Party. Early in 1943 there was a last 'changing of the guard'. In spite of his ulcer Mussolini took on the Foreign Office again with Bastianini as Under-Secretary: Ciano was made Ambassador to the Vatican and it was widely hoped that he would put out peace feelers to the West. General Ambrosio succeeded Cavallero as Chief of Staff: Bottai and Buffarini-Guidi were dismissed at the same time.

Bastianini was one of many Italians and some Germans who now hoped to revivify the position of Italy and that of the Duce by again taking over in Rome the leadership of the smaller nations like Hungary and Romania in demanding guarantees of national autonomy from Germany. However when Ribbentrop came to Rome at the end of February 1943 he insisted that nothing but force would work. 'It was a typical Axis situation – the Germans insisting on the utmost brutality and a purely military "solution", while the Italians urged a political one.'[1] It was typical, too, that the Fascists still harboured some genuine respect for nationalism, a notion of no interest to the National Socialists except when it served their purposes. Hitler and Ribbentrop did, however, realise that Italians, Romanians, Hungarians were longing to escape from the war, and they decided on verbal concessions to Bastianini and the Duce. On 1 March it was

indeed broadcast from Berlin that during his visit to Rome
Ribbentrop had

repeatedly emphasised the determination of their countries
[Germany and Italy] to continue the war with all necessary
means until the complete destruction of the enemy forces
and the elimination of the danger of a Bolshevist Europe. . . .
They [the Axis leaders] once more emphatically asserted the
resolute will of Germany and Italy to set up a new order in
Europe after achieving final victory. . . . The European
peoples will be guaranteed the possibility of productive
work and social justice within the secure frontiers of the
Great European area . . . an importance that should not be
underestimated is attached to the discussions in Rome. . . .
The Italo-German statement represents the Magna Carta
of the Great European area.

It was characteristic that in September 1942 the Secretary
of the Fascist *sindacati* at Turin had said openly at a meeting
at which many Fiat workers were present that one had no
right to treat the country's enemies other than as enemies.
Early in March 1943, a few days after the broadcasting of
the new European Magna Carta, there were serious strikes
at the big Mirafiori factory of the Fiat works at Turin. This
was the first definite and successful strike in Axis Europe,
over four months before the fall of Mussolini. Though it was
largely backed by Communists, some directors of the Fiat
works were known to sympathise with the strikers. Later
there were strikes in Milan too.

From 7 April to 10 April 1943 Mussolini made a sorry
pilgrimage to Klessheim near Salzburg to confer with Hitler,
as the two leaders of 'their revolutions' had periodically
done since the spring of 1940. Their last meeting had been in
this same Klessheim about a year earlier. Mussolini now
was obviously ill and asked to take most of his meals alone.
Bastianini made it clear, in spite of browbeating by
Ribbentrop, that Italy could not continue the war; he
referred frankly to the strikes in north Italy as one reason.
He knew only too well that Romania and Hungary with

Italian connivance were trying to evade their obligations to the Axis under the Tripartite Pact which in the autumn of 1940 they had been obliged to sign. Ribbentrop, however, was even more uncompromising than in February. 'Far be it from Germany', he said 'to wish to oppress any other country', but Churchill's broadcast of 21 March, advocating a Council of Europe after the war, had disturbed the smaller nations and this was not a moment at which to allow oneself to be weak.

At Klessheim in April 1943 Himmler, whom Mussolini consulted, told the Duce quite frankly that he had no support in Italy and advised him on his return to organise the equivalent of an Italian S.S. to make his régime both more severe and more secure. Strangely, instead of taking the lead Bastianini and the many who thought like Bastianini offered him, Mussolini rejected the Italian idea of Europe and once again chose Hitler *against* Italy and Europe. Somehow this contact with the Führer galvanised the exhausted Mussolini into a last attempt to restore Fascist purpose. Bocchini had died in 1940 and been succeeded as chief of police by Carmine Senise, who was rather less of a Fascist than Bocchini. Now on 14 April Senise was dismissed and an old, uncompromising *squadrista*, Renzo Chierici, was appointed in his place.

More important was the appointment of a new Secretary of the Fascist Party. Starace had gone in 1939, and his successors, Muti and Vidussoni, had been ineffectual. On 17 April, a bare week after his return from Klessheim, Mussolini summoned the Party Directorate to the Palazzo Venezia and announced that he had chosen Carlo Scorza as Vidussoni's successor.

I am certain [the Duce declared] that he will carry out my directives in a true fighting spirit. . . . In order to indicate what these directives will be, I must refer to recent happenings – to be precise, to the happenings of March 10th, the date of the disturbances among the workers in Turin,

Milan and other smaller cities of Piedmont and Lombardy. This unpleasant and deplorable incident has suddenly plunged us twenty years back. . . . We must recognize that the Party was not in command of the situation. . . . Why not? Because the Fascists themselves were not unanimous in their behaviour. Some went on strike, some did not, some made an agreement with the strikers. . . .[2]

After his usual grumbling over the middle class and what was to become an habitual statement about all wars inevitably being unpopular, Mussolini made clear that Italian Fascism must create its own S.S. in order to purge and strengthen the Fascist régime.

Scorza was a Calabrian who had, however, been a leading *squadrista* at Lucca from the beginning of Fascism. He 'now charged into his task. The Party cadres were shaken up and in the following weeks four senior Party Officers and twenty provincial Secretaries had been changed.'[3]

On 3 May Mussolini addressed the new Party officials about his new directives. Two days later Scorza spoke to a mass reunion of Fascists in the Teatro Adriano in Rome. 'The necessity of defending the country has delayed the Fascist construction,' he said. There was now a need to return to the origins of the Revolution. The Party was the link between the state and the people. 'If we must die let us swear to fall in style.'* A police report of this time said: 'The Party has in twenty years lost the confidence and esteem of even its own followers, because of the excessive robberies by the bosses and the patent injustices which have been committed.' After Scorza's speech Mussolini addressed the crowds from the notorious balcony of the Palazzo Venezia for the first time since he had declared war in June 1940. This on 5 May 1943 was 'the last public expression of the twenty-year dialogue between the dictator and the crowd'.[4] The Italian surrender in Tunisia followed almost immediately.

* 'cadere in bellezza' were the original words, literally 'to fall in beauty'.

On 7 June 1943 Scorza offered a private report to Mussolini. He was probably perfectly sincere when he wrote: 'I know you demand of me not a passive obedience so much as a faithful and mystical interpretation of your directives: rather a subordinate and intelligent collaboration founded on the assumption of the most complete sense of dedication.' He then proceeded to indict the educated classes, the Civil Service and particularly the Ministries of the Armed Forces, but of course the Minister for the Army had for many years been Mussolini. When Scorza initiated disciplinary measures the higher officials he aimed at were protected by the Minister concerned, or by the under-secretaries where Mussolini was the Minister. Indeed, as Mr Deakin has written: 'Italian Fascism had never succeeded in being totalitarian and its fate in the end was to be decided in those enclaves which it had failed in twenty years to penetrate and control – the Court, the Army, the Civil Service and even the Police.'[5] It has been seen that the judges, too, had not been flattened into total Fascism.

It may be said that Scorza did his best although rumours that he was strongly influenced by Farinacci injured his popularity. On 11 June twenty-four prefects were dismissed, a further nineteen retired, and twenty new appointments made in the provinces, all by the authority of Mussolini, who was Minister of the Interior. But on the same day the Italian naval and air base of Pantelleria fell to the enemy, who was thus on the threshold of Sicily.

As for the plan to create an Italian S.S., the M Division, this also functioned too late and only increased existing tensions. Although the Fascist Militia had been officially incorporated into the armed forces when Italy entered the war in June 1940, the Blackshirt Militia units had remained separate in practice: it was intended to use Militia men back from Russia and Croatia to form the M Division. At the end of May the Germans sent thirty-six Tiger tanks and thirty-three instructors and it was hoped that the division would be ready by the end of June under General Losana, an old Fascist. Marshal Caviglia noted in his Diary on 29 May: 'In the ranks of the Party leadership they are not preparing to overcome the foreign foe, but the internal enemy.' To men like Caviglia and Ambrosio this was all part of the unacceptable pressure of the Germans against the Italian regular armed forces and the Monarchy. It was in fact not until the Allies were landing in Sicily in July that Mussolini inspected the new M Division, trained by the S.S., near Lake Bracciano: 'It made a good impression but a brief one', and in fact never functioned at all. At a last meeting of the Council of Ministers on 19 June, two Ministers (one of whom was Cini) had the courage to demand 'a more open and frank division of responsibility', but Mussolini's only reply was 'any discussion is useless. Italy has only one alternative: to conquer or fall at the side of Germany.'

The weakness of Fascism thanks to the so-called Diarchy of Duce and King was well illustrated when Bonomi had visited Victor Emmanuel on 2 June and pointed out that if the King dismissed Mussolini, which he had a constitutional right to do at any time, the Axis alliance would no longer be valid, since the Steel Pact, according to its own preamble, was not an alliance between states but 'between two régimes and two revolutions'. Hitler had seen to it since Hindenburg's death that there was no possible distinction between the German state and the Nazi régime.

With the crisis of the invasion of Sicily things became of course far more strained: Mussolini clamoured for German help, but, in order to protect his own prestige, wished it to be under Italian control; this the Germans, with their growing doubt of Italian loyalty, were naturally unwilling to allow. They had, moreover, to defend themselves against an imminent Russian offensive.

Scorza now hoped to carry the Duce's message of a 'granite sense of decision' to the provincial capitals through a speaking tour of Party bosses, but Grandi and Federzoni refused to perform. The most independent of the Fascist leaders, Italo Balbo, had been banished to Libya, as we have seen, and had perished in a mysterious air accident on 28 June 1940 when he was apparently shot down in error by the Italians. Bottai and Bastianini, however, supported Grandi. More and more insistently Mussolini was urged to call together the Fascist Grand Council, which had not met since December 1939. He agreed to do so at a meeting of Fascist leaders on 16 July. On 19 July, by Hitler's command more or less, Mussolini met the Führer at Feltre near Treviso. Hitler was already saying that only 'barbaric measures', by which he meant wholesale executions, could now save Italy. At Feltre Mussolini scarcely opened his mouth while Hitler declaimed, sure in the belief in his new secret weapons. The Duce dared not suggest, even if he wished to do so, that the Axis alliance be abandoned. But unless it was, Mussolini's relation to his own people was injured beyond repair. Hitler was determined to maintain Mussolini as the Fascist figurehead and believed that Farinacci was acting in Rome against the possibility of an anti-Fascist *coup d'état* by pressing for the Grand Council to meet.[6]

By the end of the week, that is on Saturday, 24 July, at 5 p.m. the twenty-eight members of the Fascist Grand Council assembled in the Palazzo Venezia: Mussolini naturally presided. Grandi proposed a motion in favour of 'the immediate restoration of all State functions, allotting to the King, the Grand Council, the Government, Parliament and the Corporations the tasks and responsibilities laid down by our statutory and constitutional laws'. He really went back to the Fascism of the days of the semi-independent 'ras'. 'The real enemy of Fascism is the dictatorship. From the day when the old motto "Liberty and Fatherland" inscribed on the banners of the Action Squads was replaced by the other, "Believe, obey, fight", Fascism was finished.' Turning to the Duce and echoing the young Balbo, he said:[7]

'It is not enough that you assume the responsibility. We are also in it, and so is the country. . . . In the fifteen years in which you have held the offices of state, what have you done? The initiative of the Crown has been suffocated and its prerogatives manhandled.' The sentiment of the Grand Council was fairly clearly with Grandi, who knew that he had the King's approval. He had also forewarned Mussolini about his motion.

Farinacci put forward a not dissimilar motion, demanding the restoration of their functions to the bodies Grandi had listed but also to the Fascist Party. But his biggest complaint was that Italy was too independent of Germany in the military sphere and he proposed that the Italian Army leaders be called to account with the implication that Hitler's 'barbarous measures' should be employed against them. Thus Farinacci's view was diametrically opposed to that of Grandi, as it always had been. Scorza also put forward a motion advocating the formation of a Front of National Union. Mussolini seemed unable to defend himself, grumbling intermittently over the greed and squabbles of party bosses. Nineteen votes were cast for Grandi's motion and seven against, Farinacci sticking to his own formula and not voting. At 2.40 a.m. on Sunday, 25 July 1943 Mussolini rose to leave, saying to the Grand Councillors: 'You have provoked the crisis of the régime.' The only people who had supported the Duce in the voting were Scorza; Tringali-Casanova, President of the Special Tribunal; Galbiati, the commander of the Militia; Biggini, successor to Bottai as Minister of Education; and Buffarini-Guidi, now out of office, who had wanted to arrest all the others.

Although obviously shaken, Mussolini decided on his course of action apparently without difficulty. In February 1939 he had said to the Grand Council that 'an autocratic and totalitarian régime . . . should have the courage of auto-criticism', and years before he had laid down that there would never be any question of voting in the Grand Council.

Hence Grandi's motion could by his interpretation be happily ignored. In its place he, the Duce, must adopt a wild optimism and persuade Hitler to come to terms with Stalin so that the German armies could be transferred from the Russian front to the Mediterranean: there would also be Germany's secret weapons. At the same time the King might resume command of the armed forces and accept another reshuffle of ministers, Mussolini himself emerging 'triumphant, supreme and alone at the summit of power'.[8] But the Grand Council which the Duce had created as his own instrument had begun to edge him out of power.

It happened, however, that the King had prepared a plan with General Ambrosio to dismiss and arrest Mussolini, to replace him in the person of Marshal Badoglio and to prevent counter-action by an occupation of Rome by the Army supported by the military police or *Carabinieri*. The operation was smoothly carried out. There were about 850 arrests, including that of Buffarini-Guidi, but not of Scorza, who eluded arrest and went into hiding. On 27 July a senior Fascist official telephoned to a lady friend: 'We have avoided civil war; we have submitted to insults without firing a shot, and without reacting. Tomorrow we shall dissolve the Party, and all will be over.'[9] In fact *Fascismo* was dispelled – almost self-dispelled – tracelessly. No fragments of all those Fascist organisations survived, although pre-Fascist organisations re-emerged, the trade unions, for instance, while the corporations vanished into thin air. *Fascismo* had depended upon one man whose vitality was exhausted. It had not depended on the big capitalists, who were happy to shake it off and forget it. All that did remain, until someone painted them over, were Fascist slogans on walls saying that Mussolini was always right or that one should live dangerously.

There was, however, one man of great determination who needed the restoration of Mussolini and Fascism. Hitler could not accept the elimination of the 'sister revolution'.

He, therefore, ordered the kidnapping of Mussolini from his final internment on the Gran Sasso in the Abruzzi on 12 September, and he obliged him to set up the Neo-Fascist Republic which staggered along from its birth in September 1943 until its final collapse in April 1945. Mussolini's new state was frankly a German satellite and nothing else this time. It was controlled by the German armed forces, which moved in rapidly in September, by the German S.S. and General Leyers's economic organisation, the *Rüstungs- und Kriegsindustrieamt* or R.U.K.

Mussolini's new régime, if such it might be called, started with – from his point of view – one big advantage: it was a Republic. The King who had marred the Duce's autocracy was now the nominal ruler of Italy south of Rome which had been conquered by the Allies. The irritation of sharing power with Victor Emmanuel was over and the King could become the butt of Mussolini's Republican propaganda. But just as Fascism could never have triumphed without the King before this, now it was caught in the German net more firmly than ever.

The new Party Secretary was Alessandro Pavolini, who had earlier succeeded Alfieri at the 'Minculpop' and who proceeded to summon a Party Congress – not a Constituent Assembly as had been proposed to start with – to meet at Verona on 14 November 1943. The propagandistic emphasis was put upon the realisation of the old pseudo-syndicalistic aims at last, twenty years late.

The Trade Unions will be amalgamated in a General Confederation of Labour. All the impressive social legislation realized by the Fascist régime in twenty years remains intact. The Charter of Labour is its consecration and starting point for a further advance. Mussolini published an article on the day before the Congress of Verona met, in which he said: 'Fascism, liberated from so much tinsel which has slowed its march, and from too many compromises which were forced on it by circumstances, has returned to its revolutionary origins in all sectors, and particularly the social one.'

In point of fact no social change was possible, partly because the best men available – those who were not sent to work in German factories – had to be drafted into Graziani's new Republican Army, but most of all because the German military authorities, now in full occupation of Mussolini's Republic, blocked any socialisation as likely to diminish industrial production. These things contributed to the failure of the Fascist message to evoke response. At the Verona Congress there were many former *squadristi* and a certain number of younger people who had been through the Party youth formations and the G.U.F. courses. But already the best people were joining partisan bands in the mountains in the north which encircled the new seat of Mussolini's government on Lake Garda; already the neo-Fascists had a sense of being besieged by the Partisans. 'The battles of 1920–21 were to be fought out again twenty years later. . . . The partisan bands of 1943 were the successors of the victims of the Fascist squads, and situations were to be inexorably reversed.'[10]

How far does an analysis of *Fascismo* require an account of the Italian anti-Fascists? It only perhaps requires it to be said that Italian anti-Fascist exiles in France, the United States and elsewhere, had on the whole, in spite of exiles' quarrels, given a good account of themselves. The young poet, Lauro De Bosis, had thrown away his life in 1931 in order to drop anti-Fascist leaflets on Rome from an aeroplane he had scarcely learnt to control. The anti-Fascist Italians had shown up well in the Spanish Civil War. Carlo Rosselli, the hero together with Parri of the Savona trial in 1927, had been murdered in France in such a way as to advertise his martyrdom. His spiritual heirs joined with the Communists to create a clandestine press in northern Italy now. It was Rosselli's friends who called the budding resistance to Mussolini the Second Risorgimento, and founded their new Party of Action to be devoted to Rosselli's aims of *Giustizia e Libertà*. Often the Allies furnished the Italian Partisans with

D

weapons, but the Partisans fought to re-create a free Italy independent of the British, Americans or Russians.

In the early days of Mussolini's Republic of Salò there was an occasional flavour, curiously enough, of the early Fascism of a Bottai, of Fascism with 'internal criticism'. But a necessity was felt by the Duce in January 1944 to execute those members of the Grand Council who had voted for Grandi's motion in the previous July. Only six of them could be brought into court because only six of them were in the territory of Mussolini's new Republic. In the end Cianetti, who had been Minister of Corporations, was sentenced to thirty years' imprisonment; the rest – De Bono, one of the quadrumvirs of October 1922, Pareschi, Minister of Agriculture, Gottardi, President of the Confederation of Industrial Workers, Marinelli and Ciano – were sentenced to death. Marinelli was a Fascist of the early syndicalist vintage who had been made a member of the Grand Council with Farinacci in 1935. As for Ciano, he was not only the Duce's son-in-law but also the son of Costanzo Ciano, the man who was to have been the Duce's heir. The savage punishment of these six men was a frantic attempt on Mussolini's part to show strength. There is no evidence of any direct pressure from Hitler over this, but clearly Mussolini hoped to impress him too. What happened was that the Duce revealed the cruelty of a petty tyrant as he never had before; his authority was undermined rather than strengthened, and any new liberal moves or even gestures were paralysed.

Thus the neo-Fascism of Mussolini now depended on a would-be tyrant who was older, less flexible, less healthy and almost completely disillusioned. To have executed his son-in-law did not loosen his dependence upon the remorseless tyranny of Hitler. Presumably he did, most of the time from September 1943 to April 1945, believe that Hitler might still win, and that a victory for Hitler offered him his only chance. Neo-Fascism's ally, however, the hero who had always sworn to preserve the Brenner frontier, was now exposed as falsehood itself, since, immediately the Germans had occupied Italy to beyond Rome, he had annexed the Alto Adige as well as Trieste. When Mussolini went a third time to Klessheim in April 1944 to meet Hitler he protested rather helplessly. Hitler replied that these operational zones were crucial to the German strategists:[11] Mussolini was thus revealed as powerless to protect Italy's frontiers, won in 1918, from his chosen ally; this was the final result of Fascist foreign policy. Before Mussolini left Klessheim for the last time Hitler consoled him by saying:

Italy was the first, and even to-day the only one, of our allies who was closely bound to us in ideology. That was why the Führer in his own interest understandably and naturally wanted to fulfil all the wishes of the Duce. . . . The Duce and himself were certainly the two best hated men in the world, and in case the enemy got hold of the Duce, they would carry him off with a cry of triumph to Washington. Germany and Italy must win, otherwise both countries and peoples would perish together.[12]

The Republic of Salò was in fact ruled by the German military and police authorities, and depended most of all upon the S.S. General Karl Wolff, whose major task, which he failed to perform, was to destroy the Italian Partisans, or patriots as they were often called now.

In July 1944, and again on a tiny scale in December, Mussolini made brief sorties from his base at Gargnano on Lake Garda. In the first half of that year people began to doubt whether the Duce was still alive but now he went off to inspect the Italian divisions training in Germany. 'The physical presence of the Duce had produced its old hypnotic effect, and, for a moment, stirred and restored his faith in himself. He had a deep need for such emotional contacts with the crowd. . . .'[13] He then proceeded to meet Hitler at his East Prussian headquarters at Rastenburg and had the satisfaction of arriving on 20 July, the occasion of treason in

Germany – Italy proved not to have been the only Axis
partner with 'traitor-generals' and Mussolini might himself
have been caught in the trap prepared for Hitler. But the
Republic of Salò continued to bleed to death. In November
there was respite when the Allied command in Italy
instructed the Italian Partisans more or less to disperse for
the winter since the fighting in France made it impossible to
continue supplies to them. Perhaps this contributed to
Mussolini's last Duce-like moves in December when he
decided to grasp at a more real independence, to make a
public speech in Milan and to move his government to that
city where he would not be permanently encircled by the
German Army and S.S. The speech was made on 16
December with brief success and indicated that the Verona
programme of socialization would be carried out after all.
'From the social point of view', Mussolini said, 'the programme of Republican Fascism is but the logical continuation of the programme of 1919.' 'Logical' seems a curious
word for the Duce to have chosen.

By the end of 1944, however, nothing mattered any more.
Real power in Mussolini's Republic lay in the hands of
General Karl Wolff, who early in 1945 was beginning to
think in the terms of the surrender of the German Armies in
Italy which he negotiated with great difficulty in the
following months. Mussolini's last attempt to regain autonomy had no meaning in this context. When the Partisans
entered the north Italian cities in April 1945 Mussolini did
not reach the Alpine Redoubt of which he had spoken. He
was captured by Partisan officers who were not Communists, only to be handed over to a Communist, who, by
order of the Committee of National Liberation for Upper
Italy, shot him. This was the end of his Fascist fight against
Communism, the strange exercise of his own love and hatred
of it, a superficial love and hatred depending on little but
his personal thirst for power.

[1] Wiskemann, *The Rome–Berlin Axis*, p. 344.

[2] Deakin, *The Brutal Friendship*, p. 317.

[3] Ibid., p. 323.

[4] Ibid., p. 323. Mussolini did make a public speech at Milan in December 1944 but not on this scale at all.

[5] Ibid. p. 329.

[6] Ibid., pp. 420–3. Farinacci's visit to the German Embassy in Rome on 21 July confirmed Hitler's assumptions.

[7] See above, p. 25.

[8] Ibid., p. 464.

[9] Ibid., p. 475.

[10] Ibid., p. 632.

[11] Ibid., pp. 682, 687.

[12] Ibid., p. 689.

[13] Ibid., p. 707.

7 The Influence of Fascism on Hitler and National Socialist Germany

THE influence of Fascism upon Hitler was tactical rather than ideological. The anti-liberal sentiments of Mussolini Hitler could find in Austria and Germany independently; both he and Mussolini were pupils of Nietzsche. Hegel influenced many National Socialists fairly directly without the intervention of Giovanni Gentile. And many German National Socialists were really closer to Mussolini than to Hitler, never having contemplated what Hitler regarded as the necessity of destroying one's enemies physically and totally. The syndicalism absorbed into Fascism by Mussolini did not influence Hitler at all; there were no corporations in the Nazi state, only leaders of industry, though many Germans other than Hitler admired the corporative idea.

What did at first interest and impress Hitler were the tactics of the 'March on Rome' and all the techniques of Italian Fascism, especially those more gradually developed of deifying the Leader. Hitler was based on Munich at the time of Mussolini's triumph in October 1922 and he at once began to think in terms of a march on Berlin from Bavaria: indeed this was what he was trying to carry out when he planned his ill-starred Putsch just over a year later. His failure in November 1923 caused Hitler to revise his programme; after this he planned to use only 'constitutional' means to seize dictatorial power. This involved the use of open force only when one was ceasing to gain power without it – till then one became more powerful by spreading lies so monstrous that people would not recognise them. In fact Mussolini, too, had come to power constitutionally, appointed by the King.

The thing that influenced Hitler most directly about Mussolini was the way in which in October 1922 he insisted upon having the Premiership, agreeing at the same time to a coalition government drawn from many parties in which Mussolini, like many Italian Prime Ministers before him, was Minister of the Interior. He was Foreign Minister as well, but this seems to have made no particular impression on Hitler, who accepted Neurath, the Foreign Minister of Papen and Schleicher, into his own government in January 1933: after all, foreign policy had to wait in any case. What Hitler did insist upon, when he took office, was the control of the Prussian police through Goering as Vice-Premier of Prussia (nominally under Papen as Premier at first); the only other Nazi colleague he appointed at the beginning was Frick as Reich Minister of the Interior. For the rest of the grasping of real power Hitler was, like Mussolini, ready to wait a year or so. Whereas it is clear that Mussolini had not planned in advance the murder of Matteotti and the assumption of tyrannical power in January 1925, Hitler was certainly determined that his first Cabinet would be a merely transient affair, not at all the kind of government with which he would long be content. But it was a way of getting his foot in the door which would not be closed again. It should be noted that Hitler's coalition contained no liberal Catholic or Socialist elements.

Hitler – and Goebbels – were profoundly impressed with the salutes, uniforms and processions in Fascist Italy, most of which derived from d'Annunzio: to purge one's enemies with castor oil delighted them. Hitler took far less time to establish Goebbels as Minister for 'The Enlightenment of the People and Propaganda' than Mussolini took to set up his 'Minculpop'. The whole conception of the all but divine leader first displayed in Italy from about 1926 onwards was welcome to Hitler who then still had nearly seven years to wait for power. The suppression of the trade unions and of the press, and the establishment of a Special Tribunal, were all things that Hitler would imitate, and the ruthless centralisation of the national state.

The Storm Troopers or S.A. are usually regarded as Hitler's *squadristi* but it should not be forgotten that the *squadristi* were a more or less chance development of the *Arditi* into people who carried out acts of violence and gained power by intimidation. Hitler insisted that he founded the S.A. with a more specific political aim, although intimidation was their chief purpose, too: but they were far from being just the men left over from the *Freikorps*. And yet, when he wished to assume totalitarian power, Hitler on 30 June 1934 more or less liquidated these Storm Troopers of his as too amateurish. By this time Himmler had built up the S.S., a much more elaborate *élite* affair which could be trusted to be completely ruthless. Special boarding-schools, such as one never heard of in Italy, prepared specially bred boys to go into the S.S. Gradually it developed an army of its own, the *Waffen S.S.*, which competed with the *Wehrmacht*. Mussolini turned his *squadristi* into the Fascist Militia which competed with the Italian Army, as we have seen, inconsistently and ineffectually. When at Klessheim in April 1943 Himmler pointed out to Mussolini that he needed an Italian S.S., which he lacked, Himmler was acknowledged to be right because Italy had nothing comparable. For the ideology of Hitler's National Socialism, although he sometimes denied this, was distinct from that of Fascism. Hitler believed that the superior German race should annihilate or enrol as slaves the inferior Slavs and Jews, who lived in eastern Europe, in order to take their place, establishing an empire ruled by, and solely in the interests of, the superior Germans. Nothing Mussolini said or did about his new Roman Empire was comparable with this. Moreover, once war had made it possible, Hitler proceeded to carry out this programme, having, with Himmler's help, created the machinery of the S.S., men deliberately brutalised to realise these aims of Hitler's.

Hitler had also, when he launched the Second World War, groups of German settlers, derived from the earlier German minorities in non-German countries waiting ready. After endless speeches about the sacred character of the soil, the *Boden*, from which the German tribes sprang, Hitler's aims turned out to have required the uprooting of any Germans whose home or *Boden* did not lie where Hitler for the time being found expedient. He drove out, or rather allowed to be driven out, the Germans who had lived for generations in the Baltic States, Bessarabia and the Bucovina and resettled them in western Poland. The most treacherous thing Hitler did was to guarantee the Brenner frontier for ever, agreeing with the Italian authorities in the summer of 1939, that the German-speaking South Tirolese could opt to become German citizens. This seemed to emphasise the renunciation of a racial claim to the territory of the Alto Adige. The Tirolese had long supplied a high proportion of racial extremists. They were bewildered by the betrayal of their *Blut und Boden* by the arch-racialist, particularly when they discovered that they might become German colonists outside Germany. On the whole the South Tirolese had nursed a belief that Hitler would only betray them temporarily. In 1943 this turned out to be true. The South Tirol became German and Hitler betrayed Mussolini. In this case it would be rash to suggest that Hitler had planned what he did in advance – on the contrary, although not unforeseeable, this may have been a brilliant piece of opportunism. But the colonisation of eastern Europe, including much of European Russia, to create a Greater German Empire ruled by and for a superior German caste at the expense of the indigenous, was dogma to Hitler from at least 1924 onwards. Mussolini's vague mouthings about the new Rome bore no relation to this. As for the South

Tirol, the Italians in 1939 only wanted to get rid of a few unruly Nazis there; it did not occur to them to wish to expel all physiological aliens as the Germans expelled Poles and Jews from western Poland when this was annexed by Hitler. The most extreme Fascists had only wanted to italianise, that is to impose the Italian language.

An important weapon in Hitler's armoury was the Nazi concentration camp, which was consciously aimed at the humiliation and demoralisation, sometimes the annihilation, of his opponents, even of his critics. To be sent to the islands, Lipari, Ustica, in Fascist Italy was usually a fairly horrible experience, but it was not part of a systematic plan. The guards were not always inhuman, close relatives were allowed to join the prisoners and most people survived the experience – it was disagreeable rather because of the inefficiency of authority than made efficiently frightful on principle. Gramsci could never have written his letters from prison[1] had his prison been a Nazi one. It had suited Hitler in many ways to speak of Mussolini's as the 'sister revolution' and sometimes he liked to speak of the Duce as his only friend. But there were moments, even before July 1943, when he admitted, for instance to Rauschning, that Mussolini had no understanding of Hitler's revolution of human destruction.

From the beginning Fascism was caught up in the dilemma presented to it by the Monarchy. Mussolini came to power because the Monarchy and the Army allowed it. The Fascist Militia never took the place of the Army divisions nor of the police which Bocchini succeeded in keeping separate from the Fascist Party: even the Civil Service in Italy, like the judiciary, was not uniformly Fascist, perhaps because its members could feel they were serving the King rather than the Duce. The Militia was never developed into being the backbone of the Fascist state as the S.S. was the backbone of Nazi Germany. The M division was only thought of at Klessheim in April 1943, too late to have any effect at all.

All along Victor Emmanuel had the right to dismiss Mussolini. Whether the King would ever have done so without the revolt in Mussolini's own Grand Council induced by defeat, it is impossible to be sure. Whether the Senate really acted as a brake, once it was well filled with Fascist nominees, is also open to doubt. At all events Hitler hastened to abolish the fragment of diarchy which existed so long as even a senile President remained head of the state in Germany. When Hindenburg died only eighteen months after Hitler became Chancellor, the Führer took care that there should be no more presidents: technically he annexed the position which in fact was never referred to again. It took him a little longer – until February 1938 – to absorb all authority over the German Foreign Office (through Ribbentrop) and over the German Army. Although he had at first been led by Contarini, Mussolini had taken over the Foreign Office himself on coming to power and later he appointed Ciano to succeed him. Mussolini, although he had often been Minister of Defence, only became Italian Commander-in-Chief on the eve of Italy's entry into the war in June 1940. Even so the King's relation to the Army irked him.

Another basic contrast between Fascism and National Socialism lay in their approach to the established Churches and religion. Mussolini made the compromise of the Lateran Pacts of 1929, accepting Catholicism as the religion of Italy; he hoped to make use of the Catholic Church for Fascist purposes, as to some extent he succeeded in doing. Hitler's Nazi creed was directly anti-Christian. Although he at first allowed some of his admirers to try to capture the Churches, in the end it was clear that compromise was impracticable. The 'German Christians', keen Nazis who broke away from the Lutheran Churches, were obviously anti-Christian. It is impossible to contemplate in Fascist Italy the official encouragement of illegitimate births which in Nazi Germany was given to the members of the S.S. at least.

The issue of anti-Semitism would probably never have

arisen in Italy had it not been superimposed upon the Fascist
scene by Hitler – indirectly of course. Even when his
influence over Mussolini was at its height the Fascists
thought at most of the segregation of the Jews somewhere
like Madagascar. There is no evidence that the idea of the
physical annihilation of the Jews crossed the Fascist mind.
This is true of many Germans who called themselves Nazis:
this is why I think many of them were rather Fascist than
Nazi. The idea of physically annihilating one's enemies
occurs in some French rightist writing and Dr Nolte has
found a British Fascist called Spencer Leese, who spoke of
'Death Chambers' for Jews,[2] but I have not found it in
Fascist 'literature': indeed it is interesting to see in Ciano's
Diary how that young tough was shocked by Nazi barbarity.*
It was this and the definition of enemies in biological terms
which made Hitler into the enemy of any form of Christianity.

The Fascists had thought they were seeking new kinds of
Hegelian freedom. To the Nazis freedom meant power, the
freedom to dominate. In nearly twice the time the Nazis
had, Fascism failed to permeate the Italian nation. The
Germans were more docile to start with and in many parts
of Germany – in much of Prussia at least – readier to accept
severe military discipline: on the face of it Nazi Germany
seemed to spell Hitler's triumph. Yet even here the dictator
had the disappointment of discovering that his people did
not welcome the war which his ideology made inevitable.

The word Fascism has been taken over by Marxists to
abuse what they regard as their class enemies: this leads to
every kind of confusion and misunderstanding, blurring the
distinctions between Fascism and National Socialism. Of
course both things were anti-Marxist, though much more
fundamentally anti-liberal.

There is certainly considerable justification for the Marxist
interpretation of the word Fascism. It has been seen that
Cini himself called Italian Fascism the last ditch of

* See *Ciano's Diary*, 4 Dec. 1939.

capitalism, which, it has been shown, made good use of Mussolini to extend its wealth and power in Italy. If Mussolini desired personal power before everything – and it may have been this desire which made his corporate state a failure in practice – all the evidence provided by what he said and wrote suggests that there was in him a modicum of genuine sympathy with notions of social justice, some understanding of the problems of poverty. It can, of course, be said that in the autumn of 1943 he went back to his early plans for socialisation simply because he thought they would be popular in the factories of northern Italy. In fact he had already alienated all the social classes of Italy by going to war in June 1940: it is of interest that the Italian industrialists were unable to prevent Mussolini from going to war.

Hitler was never the tool of the industrialists. He coaxed their money out of them in long speeches which played on the Pan-German sentiments of some of them and so gained him political power over Germany. The German industrialists were glad to have the trade unions suppressed, rearmament suited them, the destruction of Poland and the humiliation of the Czechs and the French were gratifying to them. But there were few cries of applause from big business when Hitler, in order to set up his racial empire, attacked the home of Communism, the U.S.S.R. Probably from this time onwards the capitalists of Germany deplored the Führer's actions, but they were absolutely unable to check them. Another war with the United States was the last thing any of them would have chosen, for it was sure to set the seal on their hope of resurrecting the Hohenzollern Germany for which they felt nostalgia.

Hitler had cared only for social injustice, the strengthening of the strong. He ended, as Golo Mann has said,[3] by causing the destruction of the old social framework of Germany. Above all his career helped to destroy the old Junker class which had survived into the Weimar period, paralysing the Republic. Ralf Dahrendorf calls this the modernisation of society.[4] Fascism in Italy made a much smaller contribution to this.

It seems true to say that if Mussolini invented the word totalitarian, only Hitler – apart from the possible claims of Communist governments – put it into practice.

The question arises as to whether Hitler would have come to power in Germany if there had been no Fascist régime in Italy. This is a matter of possibly valueless conjecture, but it seems certain that Hitler would have known how to grasp power in Germany without the example of Mussolini. He would have known how to offer everything to everyone and how to find financial support and how to propitiate the leading figures in the German Army. The German Communists would have helped to bring Hitler to power by deriding the Social Democrats if there had been no Mussolini. And if he had come to power without the Duce's example to seem to follow, his régime, which diverged from that of Mussolini in so many ways, would have been the very same racial tyranny that it became.

It is an extraordinary fact that, whereas Italian Fascism did not speak of the dominance of the Italians exclusively and therefore could serve as a model to non-Italians in theory, German National Socialism, which aimed at a German racial empire supposedly unacceptable to non-German nationalists, had more direct influence in other countries. It will be seen that it influenced them through anti-Semitism and grossly deceptive propaganda, in spite of the fact that its actual performance could not well be accepted by non-Germans as an example. There were, however, many Germans outside Germany, first and foremost the Austrians.

[1] A. Gramsci, *Lettere del carcere.*

[2] E. Nolte, *Die faschistischen Bewegungen*, p. 280.

[3] G. Mann, *The History of Germany since 1789*, pp. 524–5.

[4] R. Dahrendorf, *Society and Democracy* (1968).

8 Fascism and Austria

WHEN the first Austrian Republic was established and the Peace Treaties vetoed the Anschluss in 1919, the Pan-German indignation of the more conservative Austrian Germans exceeded all bounds. They could not forgive the Austrian Social Democrats for accepting the Treaty of Saint-Germain, and their anti-Marxist indignation was immense. They volunteered to join the *Heimatschutz* to which the government issued arms, as it did to Socialist volunteers, so that order should be preserved and the frontiers, especially on the Yugoslav side, be protected. The *Heimatschutz* was the same kind of thing as the *Freikorps* in Germany. In the west of Austria the right-wing volunteers acquired the name of *Heimwehr* and were in close touch with the seething mass of right-wing groups in Bavaria.

Through the Christian-Social politician, a South Tirolese called Richard Steidle, the *Heimwehr* established some kind of contact with Seipel's clerical or, more precisely, Christian Social, party. In eastern Austria the people on the right at first formed the *Frontkämpfer* Association. It was in a clash in the Burgenland in January 1927 between *Frontkämpfer* and the members of the Socialist *Schutzbund* that a number of Socialist casualties resulted. In July 1927, when the *Frontkämpfer* responsible were acquitted in Vienna, riots ensued and the law-courts were burnt down. From this time onwards democracy faltered and collapsed in Austria, playing into the hands of the rightist anti-democrats.

The situation was in some ways like that in the Weimar Republic: a big capital city inclined to the left was confronted by a country population with right-wing inclinations. The situation was in some ways more acute than in

Germany because in Austria the only massive urban population was in Vienna where the Socialists were in charge. But the Catholic Church was strong in Austria, and the anti-clericals were divided between the German Nationalists (who joined the *Heimwehr*) and the Social Democrats. Hence the Christian-Social leader, Dollfuss, who was neither a Fascist nor a Nazi, was to try in 1934 to substitute for the democratic republic which had been reduced to deadlock, a corporate state fundamentally based upon Leo XIII's Encyclical of 1891, the *Rerum Novarum*. This was reinforced by Pius XI in his Encyclical, the *Quadragesimo Anno*, of May 1931.

In point of fact the ideology of the Austrian Right was not so simple as this might imply. Although the word Fascist crept into the Austrian vocabulary, the Austrian Right was not originally influenced by Mussolini. There was a negative reason for this, contempt for Italy and everything Italian and a bitter resentment of the persecution of the German-speaking population of the South Tirol by Mussolini. But there was a positive reason too, the influence of Professor Othmar Spann of the University of Vienna. Spann believed in organic – in German, *bündisch* or *ständisch* – groupings, in a vaguely back-to-the-guild medievalism which was related to Leo XIII's Encyclical. Into the bargain Spann believed in a resurrection of the Holy Roman Empire of the German Nation, a chain of German guilds or *Stände* in control of all central and eastern Europe. Spann's *magnum opus* was first published in Germany in 1921 and had thus been written almost before Fascism existed recognisably in Italy. It was called *Der wahre Staat*, praised *élites* and evoked rapid response in the right-wing world of Austria, and also – the same thing – among the Germans of Czechoslovakia many of whose leaders studied in Vienna. Spann and Steidle met for lectures and discussions at the German Club in Vienna where representatives of the German *Stahlhelm* joined them.

Although the *Heimwehr* began with strong antipathy

towards Italy, Mussolini himself took much interest in its success. His renegade's hatred of Socialism was especially directed against the 'Austro-Marxists' of Vienna. From the time of his *rapprochement* with Hungary in 1927 he and Bethlen conspired together with the ultimate object of destroying the Austrian Socialists. For Bethlen the latter had the vices of being allied in interest with the Czechs and an encouragement to the Hungarian Socialists whom Bethlen allowed only half to exist, hampered as they were by the Hungarian police. The beginning of the Italo-Hungarian friendship just preceded the burning down of the law-courts of Vienna. From this time onwards the *Heimwehr* found themselves able to accept payment from the Italian dictator and to adopt many of his habits, especially to express all possible abuse of both Marxism and democracy. Even before this, in May 1926, with the first news of Mussolini's corporate state, the west Austrian paper, the *Alpenländische Heimatwehr*, had expressed approval of Mussolini's *corporazioni* which would avoid 'serious economic conflicts'.

Four years later in May 1930 at Korneuburg in Lower Austria a conference of *Heimwehr* leaders adopted what they called the Korneuburg oath. It was a repetitive affair.

We repudiate [it said] western parliamentary democracy and the party state.

We are determined to replace them with government by the corporations (*Stände*) and by a strong national leadership which will consist, not of the representatives of the parties but of leading members of the large corporations and of the ablest, most trustworthy men in our own mass movement.

We are fighting against the subversion of our *Volk* by Marxist class-struggle and liberal and capitalist economics. . . .

The state is the personification of the whole *Volk*. . . .

Let every comrade realize and proclaim that he is one of the supporters of a new German national outlook, namely: that he is prepared to offer up his blood and his possessions, and that he recognizes three forces only: Faith in God, his own unbending will, the commands of his leaders.

In fact the right-wing Austrians were in an Austrian dilemma, for their nationalism, their *Volk*, was German, and they did not wish to be Austrian – in other words they were Pan-German and dreamt of German union. But by themselves they were helpless and the only help that was offered them came from Italy, regarded as a national enemy on account of the war and still more on account of the South Tirol.

And so, in spite of the inflow of lire, the *Heimwehr* lost ground. It did not do well in the Austrian elections of November 1930, and from 1932 onwards it was gravely undermined by the growing force of the Austrian Nazis who were younger Pan-Germans paid, not by Italy, but by Germany. The *Heimwehr* had never been very consistent or uniform in its ideology and it was made less so by the confusing figure of Prince Starhemberg. In his early days he had been a *Freikorps* man and all but a Nazi. He then developed ambitions to help rule an independent Austria of which no Nazi could approve. Having attached himself to Dollfuss's Christian-Social Party Starhemberg became Mussolini's 'homme de confiance' in Austria. But the *Heimwehr* was killed by its Italian patronage which played straight into the hands of the Nazis.

Dollfuss was not authoritarian or Fascist by nature. He was faced by a political impasse at home, by the Great Depression, by the studied distrust of the Socialists who foolishly opposed the loan offered to Austria at the Conference of Lausanne in 1932. In January 1933 the Austrian Socialists discovered and made public that Mussolini was sending material to the Austrian arms factory at Hirtenberg, partly to be used by the *Heimwehr* and partly to be sent on to Hungary. So Dollfuss was urged by Mussolini, by the Hungarian Premier, Gömbös, and by the *Heimwehr* to suppress the Socialists which he at last did in February 1934. Then in May 1934 he launched the Patriotic Front which appealed to all Austrians to unite under Dollfuss against

Hitler. Under the aegis of the Patriotic Front Dollfuss tried to transform Austria into a corporate State, more medieval and submissive in tone than Mussolini's because of the preponderant influence of the Church.

Yet the régime Dollfuss established, authoritarian and clerical though it was, was far from totalitarian. Differing political groups survived and, for instance, Ernst Karl Winter, a democratic left-wing Catholic, was appointed Vice-Mayor of Vienna in the post-Socialist government of that city. Indeed opinion remained relatively free while Austria survived, for one could openly express any views other than Marxist and Nazi ones. In fact many people were more intimidated by fear of a future Nazi régime than of Dollfuss's rule, while in Styria in south-east Austria Nazi views and expectations were expressed without hesitation.

When the Austrian Nazis murdered Dollfuss in July 1934, Mussolini's mobilisation appeared to safeguard Austria's survival though it was welcome fuel to the flames of Nazi propaganda.

Dollfuss's successor, Schuschnigg, carried on the struggle to establish the Patriotic Front. He accepted Starhemberg as a colleague to ensure the support of what remained of the *Heimwehr*. But in February 1936, in the crisis of the Abyssinian war, Starhemberg sent the following telegram to Mussolini:

In the consciousness of the close bonds of sympathy which involve me as a Fascist in the destiny of Fascist Italy, I congratulate Your Excellency with all my heart both in my own name and in the name of all those who are fighting for the triumph of the Fascist idea, on the glorious and wonderful victory of Italian Fascist arms over barbarians, on the victory of the spirit of Fascism over dishonesty and hypocrisy, and on the victory of Fascist devotion and disciplined determination over mendacious demagogy. Long live the clear-sighted leader of victorious Fascist Italy; may the Fascist idea triumph throughout the world![1]

Schuschnigg could not accept this denigration of the League of Nations upon which Austria still depended financially: hence he dismissed Starhemberg from his government. Thus Schuschnigg rejected the identification of Austria's interest with that of Fascist Italy. This may have contributed to the waning of Mussolini's support of Austrian independence, and therefore, possibly, to the Anschluss. But at any rate it cannot be maintained that Italian Fascism had much direct influence upon the shape of the government of Austria, although it appeared to do so and bore a large part of the responsibility for the suppression of the 'Austro-Marxists'. Dollfuss's 'shooting down of the workers' was marvellous grist to the Nazi mill, and so Italian Fascism helped to make the Austrians readier for Hitler.

Thus the tenuous influence of Italian Fascism in Austria was driven out by the influence and power of Hitler.

[1] See Ludwig Jedlicka, 'The Austrian Heimwehr', in *Journal of Contemporary History*, vol. 1, no. 1, 1966.

9 Eastern Europe

GERMANY and Austria apart, the influence of Italian Fascism was probably weaker than has often been supposed. In the 1920s Mussolini and Fascist Italy were the novelty of the day. He was a good performer and people at home and abroad enjoyed the show: it even linked up with modern art via futurism and thus seemed attractive to Wyndham Lewis and Ezra Pound, and, for slightly different reasons, to Bernard Shaw. When democracy broke down in a politically and economically immature society like that of Poland in 1926, people liked to say that Poland had 'gone Fascist' and that Pilsudski was another Mussolini. This confused the issues. Under Pilsudski Poland was ruled much as Eastern Europe had traditionally been ruled before 1914. It did not become totalitarian, for oppositional groups could continue to exist, if uncomfortably. Nor did Pilsudski play the national God. The same thing was roughly true of Yugoslavia and of Romania before 1938. Among the Czechs and Slovaks only the odd freak was attracted by Italian Fascism, the clerical Slovaks later feeling some sympathy for the Austria of Dollfuss and Schuschnigg. The Germans of Czechoslovakia went much further: it has been seen that some of their leaders were disciples of Spann, but Henlein, though he concealed it for years, was really a fervent admirer of Hitler.*

The warring nationalities of the Habsburg Empire had made the Danubian peoples more conscious of race since at least 1848, and thus more aggressively racial than most Germans were before Hitler except when they spoke of the Poles. The natural anti-Semitism of eastern Europe, induced

* J. W. Brügel, *Tscheche und Deutsche* (1967).

partly by the lack of a non-Jewish middle class, caused the
east Europeans to be more impressed by Hitler's anti-Semitic
creed than by Mussolini. National Socialism was more
folkloristic and peasanty than Fascism, and this also had
more appeal in the predominantly peasant countries. The
German minorities scattered across eastern Europe took up
National Socialism with zeal; it was largely through them,
and the Nazi agents who visited them, that the east
Europeans were made familiar with the more publicised of
Hitler's tenets – there were no Italian minorities in eastern
Europe.

In spite of Mussolini's official friendship with Hungary
from the time of the Treaty of April 1927 and in spite of the
fitful Magyar study of the Fascist régime, the influence of
Italian Fascism in Hungary was slender and superficial. The
Hungarians were part of central Europe where German
cultural influence, whether one liked it or not, had been
strong for centuries.

Many Hungarians had some familiarity with the German
language, and post-Trianon Hungary had an important
German minority of half a million. Industry was still
backward, there was only one big town which in 1848 had
still been three-quarters German, and the functions of an
urban middle class were to a considerable extent fulfilled by
Jews. The Magyars were obsessed by their desire to revise
the Treaty of Trianon in their own favour, and in the late
twenties and early thirties they hoped Mussolini would
contribute to this purpose. Their grave social problem,
however, although the ruling classes tried to conceal this,
was the problem of their three million landless labourers out
of a population of nine million altogether.* In other words
the land of Hungary was still owned mainly in large and
medium-sized estates by the magnates and squires who had
successfully resisted anything but a nominal redistribution of

* Between two and three million Hungarians lived as minority com-
munities in the neighbouring countries.

property, grumbling over the estates they had lost in Slovakia and Transylvania. The result was that Hungary constituted the, rurally, most backward country in eastern Europe west of Turkey, with an alarmingly high proportion of poor peasants, the notorious three million, but also many others with plots which were not viable.

The Communist régime in Hungary under the Jew, Kun, had been destroyed in 1919 by Horthy and his supporters in a so-called White Terror suppressing the Red one. Indeed the Magyars regarded themselves as experts on the subject of Communism because they had experienced it. (So, oddly enough, had Bavaria more briefly.) Hence Mussolini's anti-Communism was very welcome, more particularly because Hungarian sentiment had been bitterly anti-Russian since the Czar invaded Hungary in 1849, and bitterly anti-Slav in general because the Magyars were afraid of all their Slav neighbours, many of whom they had oppressed in the past; this feeling fitted on to the Adriatic beginnings of *Fascismo* although the Magyars would have preferred Fiume to be returned to them.* But Mussolini's message in favour of a centralised tyranny in a one-party state was unwelcome to the Hungarian ruling oligarchy and to the rudiments of a middle class which liked to imitate the landed aristocracy. Of course 'strong government' was generally praised, but the impact of Fascist influence was slight and left few traces, before the influence of Hitler became strong. This reached Hungary through the half-German officer, Gömbös,† who was appointed Premier of Hungary by Horthy in 1932, but also from groups resisting the state's power. Most of all perhaps the Magyars responded to Hitler's anti-Semitism at a time when Mussolini had not thought of it.

The central figure of a Nazi–Fascist kind in Hungary (there were many of them) was the Major Szálasi whom

---

* Before 1918 the port of Fiume belonged directly to Hungary – it had done so since 1779.

† Gömbös had been strongly influenced by Mussolini before this.

Hitler at the very end of the war, that is to say in October 1944, made into the ruler of the country for that last brief period. Szálasi had published a 'Plan for the Construction of the Hungarian State' in 1933. He advocated intransigent revisionism, extreme anti-Semitism and uncompromising dictatorship. Although his ideas were ruthlessly cruel – whoever hesitated to accept his notions, he wrote, 'must be taught them with the knout' – he was not anti-religious. In so far as he and people of his kind gained importance, however, it was because they made their creed into a revolutionary demand for social justice on the land. After 1933 German Nazi propaganda fully exploited this situation, and one heard, for instance, in the summer of 1938 of Hungarian villages where the peasants were so mystically impregnated with the gospel of the swastika that they were praying that Hitler would come to give them the land. Mussolini may have meant something to the scanty Magyar middle class, but he meant nothing to the millions of Magyar peasants. As Hitler was gradually recognised as stronger and more ruthless than Mussolini he gained adherents among the Hungarian revisionists. But these were partially cancelled out by those feeling that Mussolini was less ruthless and therefore less dangerous to the independence of a smaller state.

Although Nazi influence was so effective in Hungary the fact must not be neglected that until Hitler imposed Szálasi upon the Magyars, the Horthy régime, backed by the magnates and squires as a whole, resisted the pressure from the pro-Nazi groups. In addition to Nazi activities with a seditious ring to them, Liberal and Socialist opposition on a very small scale was countenanced. The chief concession made to Nazi pressure was a certain amount of anti-Semitic legislation, of a restrictive kind, but the Jews were not in physical danger until the German occupation in March 1944 and the arrival of Eichmann.

In Romania as in Hungary pro-Fascist or pro-Nazi figures

never came to power before the Second World War; it was only a matter of subversive groups. Mussolini's attractions as a fellow Latin were diminished by his patronage of Hungarian revisionism – strongly anti-Romanian – after 1927. On the other hand Romanian patriots were very anti-Russian as well as anti-Communist, and some had been influenced through a Parisian education by some of the French right-wing writers. Codreanu, the creator of the Iron Guard in Romania, was mystically devoted to the Greek Orthodox Church which divided him from Italian Fascism. Probably the strongest force impelling Codreanu, however, was anti-Semitism. Again Nazi propagandists cashed in on this and on the poverty of the Romanian peasants. As in Hungary they created a popular belief that Hitler was the poor man's friend. In Romania there were two separate, influential German minorities by whom the idea that Hitler stood for social justice was disseminated. There was by contrast no popular awareness of Mussolini in Romania and it cannot be maintained that the influence of Italian Fascism was in any way decisive, except perhaps upon King Carol, a Hohenzollern by descent. In February 1938 he tried to solve his country's problems by establishing a one-party state based upon a 'Front of National Rebirth' with himself as dictator. The end of Codreanu, but not of his movement, came nine months later when he and some of his associates, who had been imprisoned by the King, were shot 'while attempting to escape'. King Carol had never been popular and was finally shaken off his throne by Romania's loss of territory to Hungary, according to the Belvedere awards of November 1938 and August 1940. Iron Guardists tried to take over but they soon clashed with, and were finally crushed by a professional soldier, Marshal Ion Antonescu, who presided over the government of Romania from January 1941 until his fall in August 1944. His régime might be defined as late Italian Fascist, that is, it was authoritarian, anti-Communist, anti-Slav and anti-Semitic, but not a state based upon machinery like that of the German S.S. It may be noted that Antonescu was one of the few people for whom Hitler expressed admiration although the Führer provided refuge in Germany for his Iron Guard opponents so as to be able to exert blackmailing pressure upon him.

The word Fascist in a Mussolinian sense was, of course, loosely applied to authoritarians in many places, notably to Stoyadinović in Yugoslavia. As for the Croat dictator, Ante Pavelić, whom the Axis powers installed in Zagreb in 1941, he had had his ideology all ready in that same Zagreb before 1914, independently of Mussolini or Hitler; it had to do with the alleged Gothicism of the Croat 'race'. Of course the Axis leaders taught him a little about modern techniques of propaganda and terrorisation. Similarly, French right-wing thought could be regarded as autochthonous, from Gobineau, or indeed earlier, to Maurras. Marshal Pétain's 'French State' with its capital at Vichy, was, however, authoritarian without being doctrinaire. Extremists like Doriot and Déat played no great part before the German conquest of France. On the other hand the *Comité Secret d'Action Révolutionnaire*, more popularly referred to as the *cagoulards*, were in close touch with the Italian Secret Service and supplied the murderers of Rosselli in 1937. They specifically aimed at imitating Italian Fascism in France. Both in the Netherlands and Belgium the influence of Hitler predominated over that of Mussolini. As for Quisling of Norway, he chiefly abhorred the U.S.S.R.

10 Spain, Portugal, Mosley and Switzerland

I T is often presumed that Italian Fascism strongly influenced political developments in Spain and Portugal, but the historian looking for evidence for this will find it flimsy. The apologists for General Primo de Rivera claim to find in him the influence of Chesterton, Péguy, Maritain, Sturzo. He is known to have held Ortega y Gasset to be right over the importance of *élites*, and to have approved of Maura and revolution from above. In fact Primo de Rivera was a fairly simple-minded soldier who depended entirely upon the Spanish Army in the years he ruled Spain from 1923 to 1930. He was uncritically loyal to the King. Like many military-minded people he was opposed to free trade and in favour of Spanish self-sufficiency. After Primo's fall younger men in Spain who disliked the Anarchists and the Left in general began to talk a great deal about capturing the working classes for an authoritarian, socially radical nationalism. This sounded exactly like Fascist Italy but was to a considerable extent indigenous. In October 1933 Primo de Rivera's son, José Antonio, together with Ledesma, founded the Spanish *Falange*. Its doctrine was close to Italian Fascism though its leaders were pious Catholics.* They condemned Catalan feeling because it was based upon distinctions of race and language which, they contended, offered false criteria. The Catalans they believed, should accept the Spanish nation's 'unity of destiny' – this might have been Tolomei addressing the South Tirolese. José

---

* Ledesma had originally been an atheist, but had changed.

Antonio Primo de Rivera and Ledesma wished to convert the workers to a nationalistic corporate state on the lines of Bottai's *Carta del Lavoro*, Italian influence upon them becoming considerable with time. Indeed so personally intoxicated was José Antonio with Mussolini at one point that, recalling the end of an interview with the Duce,[1] he could write:

Slowly he returned to his table to start on his task once more in silence. It was seven o'clock in the evening. . . . The Corso was all activity and gossip, like the Alcala at the same time – people going in and out of cafés and cinemas. One might think that the Duce alone remained at work, next to his reading light, in the corner of an immense empty room, keeping vigil for his people for Italy, whose breathing he could hear, heaving like an infant daughter. What apparatus of government, what system of checks and balances, councils or assemblies, could replace this picture of the Hero become Father, watching by a nightlight the toil, as well as the rest, of his people?[2]

This was, however, paternalistic rather than Fascist in its tone, and might have been written of José Antonio's father.

In April 1937 Franco, above all a soldier, united all political groups on the Nationalist side in the *Falange Española Tradicionalista de las Jons*, thus establishing his own one-party State which was possibly nearer to Primo *père*'s notions than to José Antonio's. Indeed after José Antonio's execution by the Republicans in 1936 there was little direct Italian Fascist influence although Franco's *Falange* did set up corporations not unlike those in Italy, which were bitterly hated by a large proportion of the Spanish working people. Although the Germans who fought in Spain – there were many fewer of them – were less unpopular than the Italians, there was no real Nazi influence, the power of the Church, as of the Army, now being unchallenged.

As for Portugal under Salazar, it too was authoritarian and very Catholic with a Corporate Chamber as well as a National Assembly. It had a Party Militia and a Party youth organisation. Further, Salazar's National Labour statute of 1933 was based on the Italian *Carta del Lavoro*; indeed Salazar often expressed admiration for Mussolini. Of course Italian Fascism affected the political climate, no doubt making the Portuguese readier to submit to Salazar's system. And yet Salazar himself was a retiring character, no popular tribune, and he suppressed certain more aggressive and frankly Fascist movements that attempted to launch themselves in Portugal. Thus, although Salazar survived so long, it remains true that Italian Fascism was not the conquering creed of the century, but rather a political fashion for some twenty years.

It is pointless to catalogue all the inter-war movements with a Fascist flavour in the world[3] of those days. One or two other cases, however, seem to call for mention, for instance that of Oswald Mosley. Mosley had begun as a Conservative but then became prominent in the Labour Party. Basically not unlike Mussolini in character, he was impatient of discussion or contradiction. He was attracted by Mussolini's oratorical devices, rolling his eyes as he believed the Duce did. A visit to Italy caused him to believe that Mussolini was tackling labour problems in a 'modern' way which, he, Mosley above all wished to do. But Mosley's programme owed much more to his own compatriots, particularly to Joseph Chamberlain and in part to Keynes. He did advocate a kind of corporativism but this, too, was – usually under the name of guild socialism – much discussed in the Britain of his day. His followers adopted anti-Semitism from Hitler before Mussolini did so, but Mosley himself claimed not to be anti-Semitic.

Finally the case of Switzerland deserves mention for many reasons. The Swiss consisted of a big German-speaking majority, but also of a French-speaking and Italian-speaking section with full equality of language rights in education, the law-courts and so on. Switzerland, moreover, comprised a plebiscitary but conservatively liberal democracy with an unadulteratedly individualistic, anti-Socialist economic system. It was permanently neutral by international law. Thus in every way but one it contravened the notions both of Italian Fascism and German National Socialism. The Swiss were 'plutocrats', not Communists.

In the brief period of his youth which Mussolini had spent in Switzerland he had had many a skirmish with the Swiss police and he preserved a grievance against the Swiss authorities. He often made scornful references to Switzerland in his speeches, making clear that he staked a claim to the Italian-speaking area of the Ticino centred on the cities of Locarno and Lugano. The Italian-speaking Swiss were, however, little attracted by Italian Fascism; anti-Fascist refugees often passed through the Ticino where their experiences became familiar. The exception that proved the rule was Giuseppe Motta, for many years Swiss Foreign Minister who shared Neville Chamberlain's attitude towards the dictators.

On the other hand among French–Swiss middle-class and patrician families Italian Fascism was felt to have attractions. French political literature of the Right was familiar to them and they easily admired Maurras and de la Rocque. It was interesting, however, that their disgust over the Popular Front in France in 1936 made into a favourite slogan among them 'Rather Hitler than Blum', for they were anti-Semitic and Mussolini was not enough for them in spite of Hitler's flaunting of France when he remilitarised the Rhineland in March 1936. Right-wing feeling was particularly strong in Geneva where the Socialist Mayor, Léon Nicole, elected by many near-Communist working people, caused alarm to the propertied classes. The university students of Geneva disliked what they were told from rightist sources about the League of Nations, resenting its physical presence in Geneva and claiming that it interfered with Swiss neutrality. There was a good deal of sympathy with Mussolini, and anti-League feeling, over Abyssinia.

This was true, too, in German-speaking Switzerland. A leading member of the staff of the most important German–Swiss newspaper had an undeniable weakness for Mussolini which was to some extent pervasive. But here the Duce's attraction was chiefly exotic. It was National Socialism which came close to the German-speaking Swiss, in their own language or the written version of it. For a time it was rather the vogue for young people to join fairly blatantly Nazi 'fronts' – it was part of the revolt of the young against the almost rigid conservatism of the older men who governed Switzerland and controlled its economic life. But soon the German–Swiss, like the Austrians, were caught up in the paradox of the Germanies. If they accepted the nationalism of Hitler they accepted the destruction of Switzerland and their own absorption into a greater Germany. As Swiss patriots most German–Swiss were soon repelled by Hitler's claims to *Gau Schweiz*. They also grasped early almost the full implications of Hitler's creed. And so, although the German–Swiss were extremely hostile to Soviet Russia and inclined to be anti-Semitic on paper, they were in the end the population least influenced by National Socialism. With their dismay over Hitler and Mussolini's growing subjection to him, the Duce lost his charm for the German–Swiss; they were not affected by the tendency in eastern and south-eastern Europe to prefer Mussolini as less alarming and as a possible intermediary between themselves and Hitler.

[1] This was in his introduction to the Spanish translation of Mussolini on *Fascismo*.

[2] Hugh Thomas, 'The Hero in the Empty Room', in *Journal of Contemporary History*, vol. I, no. I, 1966.

[3] Cf. E. Nolte, *Die faschistischen Bewegungen*; but it is not always accurate.

Conclusion

ITALIAN Fascism was not the conquering creed of the twentieth century, but led a political fashion for two decades. Outside Italy its influence was slight and within Italy short-lived. While it lasted it was a spectacular affair thanks to d'Annunzio's inventiveness and to Mussolini's exhibitionism. It had grown out of Mussolini's personal vendetta, the rage of the renegade, with the Italian Marxists whom he had led for a year or so, but who, in 1914, rejected him. Although Mussolini was far from being fundamentally repelled by Communism, his quarrel with the Italian Socialists made him almost by chance into the voice of the contemporary reaction against Communism. The Communists replied by turning the word Fascist into one of their major terms of abuse and applying it to all their enemies. It has been seen that Hitler's system was at least as different as his character was from that of Mussolini. Fundamentally Mussolini was all compromise – although he concealed this under the veneer created by his vanity and his pleasure in violence – whereas Hitler was totally uncompromising. This study is a study of Mussolini's compromises which were linked, not with the clemency of a Caesar or an Henri IV, but with the inept administration of an impressionable third-rate journalist of superficial brilliance who succeeded in fascinating many of his contemporaries.

The period of Fascist rule in Italy, even without the disaster of the Second World War, brought Italy no gains and several grave disadvantages. Liberal governments had improved the land before Mussolini and could just as well have drained the Pontine marshes. After the remarkable drive towards industrialisation under Giolitti, the Fascist period saw almost a retarding of economic development relatively – the times were hard and, of course, some progress was made in the chemical, electrical and artificial-silk industries. The earlier drive was, however, resumed after Fascism in the post-war 'economic miracle'. Even one or two sensible attempts in the Fascist period to make the Italians more orderly – for instance, instructions to keep to the right on the narrow pavements of Rome – aroused a hostile reaction which has stimulated anarchical instincts ever since. Fascist education clearly spelt a relapse between the more liberal periods; even illiteracy in the south was not reduced. As between Mussolini and the Roman Catholic Church it is clear that in the end he was the loser. Indeed Italy today is everything that Mussolini would condemn. As a democracy it has worked about as well as any other in the last twenty years. As a bridge between a more oligarchic liberalism and a decentralising republic based on universal suffrage, did Fascism serve a purpose? Only one can be descried: it discredited the Monarchy and brought the Republic by default. Here alone Mussolini might have applauded his successors, but their debt was – indirectly – to Mazzini and an inheritance antithetic to Fascism in Italy.

E

Chronological Table

1883	July	Birth of Mussolini.
1896	1 March	Battle of Adowa.
1899		Foundation of *Fiat* in Turin – most important date in Italy's industrial history.
1908		d'Annunzio's dramatic poem about the foundation of Venice, *La Nave*.
1909		Marinetti's Futurist Manifesto.
1910	December	Nationalist Party founded.
1911	September	War declared on Turkey by Giolitti's government.
	October	Libya invaded.
1912	Spring	Suffrage greatly extended by Giolitti.
	May	Occupation of Dodecanese.
	June	Socialist Party Congress at Reggio Emilia.
		Left extremists carry the day: among them Mussolini becomes prominent.
	October	Italo-Turkish peace at Ouchy.
	December	Mussolini editor of *Avanti!*, the chief Socialist Party newspaper.
1913	Autumn	Election according to new voting system. Increase of Catholic, Radical and Socialist representation. Six Nationalists elected.
1914	March	Giolitti succeeded by Salandra as Prime Minister.
	June	'Red Week' in central Italy – climax of crisis between peasants and landowners.
	July–August	Outbreak of First World War.
	2 August	Italy declares neutrality.

	November	Mussolini expelled from Socialist Party: founds the *Popolo d'Italia* newspaper. *Fasci di Azione Rivoluzionaria* formed by him and other syndicalist interventionists.
1915	April	Secret Treaty of London with the Entente Powers.
	May	d'Annunzio returns from France to be the orator of the interventionists.
		Italy enters the war against Austria–Hungary.
1917	April	U.S. enters the war.
	October	Orlando becomes Premier.
	November	Italian defeat at Caporetto.
1918	April	Congress of oppressed nationalities and Pact of Rome signed by their representatives.
	Late October	Victory of Vittorio Veneto over Austria–Hungary.
	4 November	Armistice of Villa Giusti between Italy and Austria–Hungary.
1919	January	Mussolini and Marinetti break up Bissolati's meeting in Milan, because Bissolati wishes to be just to the Yugoslavs.
	23 March	Foundation of *Fasci di Combattimento* at Piazza San Sepolcro, Milan.
	24 April	Orlando leaves the Peace Conference in Paris.
	5 May	Orlando returns to Paris.
	3 June	Draft of Peace Treaty with Austria.
		Nitti succeeds Orlando as Prime Minister.
	28 June	Treaty of Versailles signed.
	10 September	Treaty of Saint-Germain with Austria signed.
	12 September	d'Annunzio seizes Fiume.

	November	General Election (universal male suffrage and proportional representation introduced beforehand). Big gains for Socialists and *Popolari*.
1920	June	Giolitti succeeds Nitti as Prime Minister.
	July	Fascist *squadristi* burn down Slovene headquarters in Trieste.
	August	Italians evacuate Valona in Albania.
	August–September	Occupation of the factories in north Italy.
	September	*Carta del Carnaro* in Fiume.
	November	Local Elections in Italy.
	7 November	Treaty of Rapallo with Yugoslavia.
	21 November	Clash at Bologna between Socialists and Fascists.
	December	d'Annunzio expelled by Giolitti's government from Fiume.
1921	January	Socialist Congress at Livorno. Gramsci breaks away to found Italian Communist Party.
	21 April	'Natale di Roma'.
	May	General Election. 35 Fascists elected.
	27 June	Giolitti resigns. Bonomi succeeds as Prime Minister.
	November	Fascist Movement becomes Fascist Party.
		Fascist Militia created to absorb *squadristi*.
1922	January	*Confederazione delle Corporazioni Sindacali* created by Michele Bianchi.
	February	Pius XI elected Pope.
		Facta succeeds Bonomi as Prime Minister.
	20 September	Mussolini in speech at Udine accepts the Monarchy.

	October	Socialist Unitary Party formed by moderate Socialists including Matteotti.
	24–26 October	Fascist Party Congress at Naples.
	28 October	Mussolini Prime Minister.
	December	Foundation of Fascist Grand Council.
1923	February	Nationalists fused with Fascists.
		Gentile's Educational Law.
		Acerbo's electoral reform.
	10 July	Sturzo resigns leadership of the *Popolari*.
	31 August	Corfu bombarded and occupied by Italians.
	27 September	Italians evacuate Corfu.
1924	January	Treaty of Rome with Yugoslavia finally brings Fiume to Italy.
	April	General Election according to Acerbo law. Great Fascist intimidation.
	30 May	Matteotti's speech condemning this.
	10 June	Murder of Matteotti.
	13 June	Aventine Secession.
1925	3 January	Mussolini's speech assuming full responsibility.
		Farinacci becomes Secretary of the Fascist Party.
		Assistance for maternity and *dopolavoro* introduced.
		'Battle of the grain' opened.
	November	Zaniboni's attempt on Mussolini's life.
	December	Ministers made primarily responsible to the Duce rather than to the King.
1926		Resignation of Contarini.
		Clash with Stresemann over South Tirol.

	April	All strikes and lock-outs forbidden.
		Balilla founded.
		Fascist calendar adopted.
	September	Bocchini Chief of Police.
	31 October	Zamboni's attempt on Mussolini's life.
	November	Special Tribunal set up.
		Treaty with Albania.
1927	April	*Carta di Lavoro.*
		Treaty with Hungary.
	September	Trial of Rosselli and Parri opens at Savona.
1928	January	Catholic Scouts suppressed.
		Gramsci condemned to twenty years' imprisonment by the Special Tribunal.
	March	New electoral law abolishes normal voting.
1929	February	Lateran Agreements signed.
	March	Plebiscitary 'election'.
		State takes over banks.
		Serpieri put in charge of land reclamation till 1935.
	June	Lateran Agreements ratified.
	December	National Council of Corporations constituted.
1930	November	Mussolini subsidises Austrian *Heimwehr* in Austrian elections.
1931		Oath of loyalty demanded from all officials.
	March	Fascist Press attacks Catholic Action.
	June	Papal Encyclical *Non abbiamo bisogno* attacks Fascism.
	September	Compromise over Catholic Youth Associations.
		I.M.I. founded.
		Starace appointed Fascist Party Secretary.
1932		Littoria founded.

	June	*Fascismo* defined in *Enciclopedia Italiana*.
	October	*Decennale*.
	November	Last Statute of Fascist Party.
1933	January	Founding of I.R.I.
		Hitler German Chancellor.
1934	February	Civil War in Austria, Socialists suppressed.
	March	Second plebiscitary vote.
		Galeazzo Ciano Under-Secretary at Press and Propaganda Office.
	June	Mussolini's first meeting with Hitler.
	July	Murder of Dollfuss.
1935	January	Laval visits Rome.
	April	Conference at Stresa.
	October	Italy attacks Abyssinia.
1936	May	Victor Emmanuel Emperor of Abyssinia.
		Bottai Minister of Education.
	June	Ciano Foreign Minister.
	July	Austro-German Agreement.
		Outbreak of Spanish Civil War.
	November	Mussolini's Axis speech in Milan.
1937		*Balilla* turns into *Gioventù Italiana del Littorio*.
	March	Battle of Guadalajara in Spain.
	June	*Ministero della Cultura Popolare* founded (= 'Minculpop').
		Murder of Carlo Rosselli.
	September	Mussolini visits Germany.
1938	March	The Anschluss.
	May	Hitler visits Italy.
	September	Czechoslovak crisis and Munich Conference.
	November	Anti-Semitic legislation introduced into Italy.
1939	February	Assembly of Corporations replaces Chamber of Deputies.
		Death of Pius XI.
		Carta della Scuola.

	March	Pius XII elected Pope.
	April	Italy seizes Albania.
	May	Steel Pact.
	September	Hitler attacks Poland. Second World War. Italy declares its non-belligerency.
1940	June	Mussolini declares war on France and Britain.
	October	Mussolini attacks Greece.
1941	April	Attack on, and partition of, Yugoslavia.
	June	Hitler attacks Russia.
	December	Pearl Harbor brings war with the United States.
1942	April	Mussolini meets Hitler at Klessheim for first time.
	November	Allies land in North Africa. Italians occupy Corsica.
1943	February	Last 'changing of the guard'. Ciano Ambassador to Holy See.
	March	Strikes at Turin and Milan.
	April	Mussolini again meets Hitler at Klessheim.
	May	Allies conquer Tunisia.
	10 July	Allies land in Sicily.
	19 July	Hitler and Mussolini meet at Feltre.
	24–25 July	Grand Council meeting.
	26 July	Victor Emmanuel dismisses Mussolini.
		The Forty-five Days.
	3 September	Italy's Armistice with the Allies. Made public 8 September.
	9 September	Neo-Fascist Republic declared by Hitler.
	12 September	Mussolini rescued by the German S.S.
	14–15 September	Mussolini sees Hitler at Rastenburg.
	23 September	Mussolini returns to Italy.
	November	Congress of Verona.

1944 January   Execution of Ciano and others.
      April   Third Klessheim meeting.
      June   Allies take Rome.
      20 July   Mussolini's last meeting with Hitler
                       (Rastenburg).
      16 December   Mussolini's last speech at Milan.
1945 28 April   Mussolini shot.

Bibliography

Very important as original material are:

I Documenti Diplomatici Italiani (*D.D.I.*), now covering much of the period.

Documents Diplomatiques Français (*D.D.F.*), published since 1964, series II. This series begins with January 1935 and documents Laval's visit to Rome in January 1935.

Documents on British Foreign Policy, 1919–1939 (*D.B.F.P.*) (H.M.S.O.).

Documents on German Foreign Policy, 1918–1945 (*D.G.F.P.*) (H.M.S.O.).

Also:

B. Mussolini, *Opera Omnia*, ed. E. and D. Susmel (36 vols., 1951–63).

Ciano's Diary, ed. with an introduction by M. Muggeridge (1947).

Ciano's Diplomatic Papers, ed. M. Muggeridge (1948).

Ciano's Diary, 1937–8, trans. A. Mayor and with an introduction by M. Muggeridge (1952).

Covering the whole topic:

Denis Mack Smith, *Italy* (1959).

As an introduction to Fascism in Italy:

B. Croce, *A History of Italy, 1871–1915* (1929).

C. J. S. Sprigge, *The Development of Modern Italy* (1943).

A. Rossi, *The Rise of Italian Fascism* (1938).

Carlo Sforza, *Contemporary Italy* (1946).

Christopher Seton-Watson, *Italy from Liberalism to Fascism* (1967). (This is particularly valuable.)

Roberto Vivarelli, *Il Dopoguerra in Italia e l'Avvento del Fascismo 1918–1922* (1967).

L. Valiani, *La dissoluzione dell'Austria-Ungheria* (1966).

On 1919:

R. Albrecht-Carrié, *Italy at the Paris Peace Conference* (1938).

On Fascist government and institutions:
  H. Finer, *Mussolini's Italy* (1935).
  G. Salvemini, *The Fascist Dictatorship in Italy* (1928).
  S. W. Halperin, *Mussolini and Italian Fascism* (1964).
  F. Chabod, *History of Italian Fascism* (1963).
  S. J. Woolf (ed.), *European Fascism* (1968).

On Church and State:
  D. A. Binchy, *Church and State in Fascist Italy* (1941).
  Richard Webster, *Christian Democracy in Italy, 1860–1960*
    (1961).
  A. C. Jemolo, *Church and State in Italy, 1850–1960* (1960).

On foreign policy:
  M. H. H. McCartney and P. Cremona, *Italy's Foreign and
    Colonial Policy 1914–37* (1938).

On relations with Hitler:
  Elizabeth Wiskemann, *The Rome–Berlin Axis*, 2nd ed.
    (1966).

On the Ethiopian question:
  George Baer, *The Coming of the Italian–Ethiopian War* (1967).
    (This is not irreproachable.)

First-rate on the decline and fall of Fascism but also on its
  earlier history:
  F. W. Deakin, *The Brutal Friendship* (1962). This book is a
    mine of first-hand information, as Mr Deakin went
    through all the available Italian and German official
    papers and has quoted them at great length. (He also
    studied all the relevant diaries and memoirs.) When I
    refer to this book I am mostly referring to the original
    Italian – or German – statements.

Biographies of Mussolini – none very good in English:
  Sir Ivone Kirkpatrick, *Mussolini: Study of a Demagogue*
    (1964). (Not always accurate.)
  Laura Fermi, *Mussolini* (1961). (A perceptive study but
    'stronger on Mussolini's personality than on his
    politics'.)
  G. Megaro, *Mussolini in the Making* (1938).
  P. Monelli, *Mussolini: an Intimate Life* (1953).

On anti-Fascism:
C. Delzell, *Mussolini's Enemies* (1961).

On opposition from within:
R. Zangrandi, *Il lungo viaggio attraverso il fascismo* (1962).

On Fascism as a general term applied to developments differing from Fascism in Italy but originally put under this heading, in order to damn them, by the Communists:
Alan Bullock, *Hitler: A Study in Tyranny* (1964).

E. Nolte, *Three Faces of Fascism* (1965). (This is good, typically Germanic theorising, but shows little feeling for the Italian atmosphere.)

E. Nolte, *Die faschistischen Bewegungen* (1966). (Not translated and not always accurate.)

Elizabeth Wiskemann, *Undeclared War* (1967). (For pro-Nazi movements in eastern Europe, but anything this book says about Italy is to be somewhat discounted as the author had not studied Italy sufficiently when the book was originally written.)

Journal of Contemporary History (1966); vol. 1, no. 1 is devoted to this whole theme.

H. Krausnick *et al.*, *Anatomy of the S.S. State* (1968).

D. Germino, *The Italian Fascist Party in Power* (1959). (Not very good.)

For Spain:
Raymond Carr, *Spain 1808–1939* (1966).
Hugh Thomas, *The Spanish Civil War* (1961).

Important books in Italian, not translated:
L. Salvatorelli and G. Mira, *Storia d'Italia nel periodo fascista* (1964).

Renzo De Felice, *Mussolini il rivoluzionario* (1965).
— *Mussolini – il conquista del potere* (1966).
— *Storia degli ebrei italiani sotto il fascismo* (1961).

A. C. Jemolo, *Chiesa e Stato in Italia negli ultimi cento anni* (1948). (The translation is abridged.)

A. Tamaro, *Vent'anni di Storia, 1922–1943* (1954). (A Fascist on the inside and of some honesty.)

G. Bottai, *Vent'anni e un Giorno* (1949).
Italo Balbo, *Diario 1922* (1932).

Index

Abyssinia, 63, 78: Wal Wal incident (1934), 58; war against (1935–6), 58, 60–1, 64, 69, 76

Accademia d'Italia, 44, 65, 73–4

Accademia dei Lincei, 73

Acerbo, Giacomo, 15

Action Squads, 12. See also *Squadristi*, 10, 11

Adriatic, the, Italian claims in, 2–5, 10

Albania: pact of Tirana (1926), 51; seized by Italy (1939), 74, 76

Alexander, King of Yugoslavia, 50–1

Alfieri, Dino (later Italian Ambassador in Berlin), head of 'Minculpop', 64–5, 88

Alpenländische Heimatwehr, 105

Ambrosio, General Vittorio, 79, 84, 87

Amendola, Giovanni, 16

Ansaldo, shipbuilding firm, subsidises Mussolini, 7, 13

Anschluss, the, 68, 103, 108

Anti-Comintern Pact, 74

Anti-Fascist influences, 47, 89–90: within movement, 47; Party of Action, 89

Anti-Semitism, 57, 68–72, 99–100, 111–12, 117: change in Mussolini's attitude, 69–70; legislation against Jews, 70, 71; in eastern Europe, 109–110

Antonescu, Marshal Ion, 113–114

Arditi, 5, 7, 8, 43, 96

Austria: Italian relations with, 52, 56–9; Fascism and, 103–108; *Heimatschutz*, 103; *Heimwehr*, 56, 103–7; *Frontkämpfer* Association, clashes with Socialists (1927), 103; Catholic Church and anti-clericalism, 104; ideology of the Right, 104; *Heimwehr* approval of corporate state, 105; Korneuburg oath (1930), 105; *Heimwehr* undermined by Nazis, 106; Hirtenberg affair, 106; Dollfuss suppresses Socialists, 106; Patriotic Front, 106–7; civil war (1934), 57–8; murder of Dollfuss, 59; Anschluss (1938), 68

Avanguardisti, 38

Avanti!, Socialist newspaper, 7

Aventine Secession, 16

Balbo, Italo, 11, 12, 14, 25: Governor of Libya, 46; death (1940), 85

Balilla (Fascist Youth organisation), 26, 28, 29, 38, 42

Bastianini, Giuseppe, 85: Under-Secretary at Foreign Office, 64, 79–81

Bauer, Riccardo, 46

Bethlen, Count Stephen, Prime Minister of Hungary, 52: intrigues with Mussolini against Austrian Socialists, 105

Bianchi, Michele, Secretary of Fascist Party, 14, 17, 22: death (1931), 46